I0762921

Memoirs of a Gay Shah

Memoirs of a Gay Shah

My STORY of FAMILY, FAME, and BECOMING A KING

REZA FARAHAN

WITH ALLIE KINGSLEY AND TONY BAKER

Cover design by Jillian Rahn/Sourcebooks
Cover images © karandaev/Getty Images, Paper Farms/
Creative Market, Replika Machine/Creative Market

This book is a memoir. It reflects the author's present recollections of experiences over a period of time. Some names and characteristics have been changed, some events have been compressed, and some dialogue has been re-created.

Published by Sourcebooks
1935 Brookdale RD, Naperville, IL 60563-2773
(630) 961-3900
sourcebooks.com

Library of Congress Cataloging-in-Publication Data

Names: Farahan, Reza author | Baker, Allie Kingsley author | Baker, Tony (Screenwriter) author
Title: Memoirs of a gay shah : my life in the Persian bubble / by Reza Farahan ; with Allie Kingsley and Tony Baker.
Identifiers: LCCN 2025020761 (print) | LCCN 2025020762 (ebook)
Subjects: LCSH: Farahan, Reza | Television personalities--United States--Biography | Gay men--United States--Biography | Iranian Americans--Biography | Gay real estate agents--United States--Biography | LCGFT: Autobiographies
Classification: LCC PN1992.4.F335 A3 2025 (print) | LCC PN1992.4.F335 (ebook)
LC record available at https://lccn.loc.gov/2025020761
LC ebook record available at https://lccn.loc.gov/2025020762

Printed and bound in the United States of America.
MA 10 9 8 7 6 5 4 3 2 1

CONTENTS

CHAPTER 1

IRAN SO FAR AWAY

It drives me nuts when I hear someone mispronounce "Iran." If I accomplish nothing else with this book, I would like everyone who reads these words to commit to never again pronouncing the country I came from as "I-RAN." I'm not a runner. I stand and fight. And I didn't run to America. I came on a plane. As a matter of fact, my family and I came here on vacation. We're actually still here on vacation, one that started in 1977 when I was four years old. If you know *Italian* is not "EYE-talian" you should also be able to handle *Iran* without this ridiculous variation.

For the record, and hopefully for the last time, it's pronounced "ee-RON."

I think this gets so deep under my skin for two reasons: One, it's lazy, and I can't fool with lazy. Google the word if you want to use it. I know you have a smartphone. Second, because nothing has made me feel like an outsider in America more than my own name. I love this country. It's been my home all these years for good reason. I've adopted the language and speak it fluently enough to handle Thomas, Robert, Jake, and any other English name you want to throw at me. Evidently, "Reza" is the most difficult two-syllable combination of sounds your average barista has ever come across. In fact, it gets on my nerves so much, when I go to Starbucks, I started giving the name "Joe" or "Nick" to avoid being "Reeza" or "RAY-za" or "RI-za." Even if I tell them the exact pronunciation while they're writing the name on my cup, it always comes back at me flipped upside down and backward. Listen when I say it. Pay attention. I'm the source. It may seem a little petty—I'm sure I'm not the only one who has ever experienced this—but to this day, that sort of thing makes me feel like people aren't paying enough attention to me to honor my place here.

I hate feeling like I don't belong, because I do. It took me a long time to realize that, though. It's not me. It's never been me. Beverly Hills simply wasn't ready for my arrival. When I was a kid, I'd walk into a toy store and my first stop would always be the roundabout displaying those mini personalized license plates. I loved those. I loved the idea of having one. I would scan the Rs every time in hopes of seeing my name. There'd be Richard, Robert, Ryan, but I could never find Reza. I was there, but I wasn't. As a kid, that hurt me deeply. It felt like rejection. There's something in that hurt that carries over when I pick up my venti iced almond milk latte with extra ice (unsweetened) and see "Joe" scrawled in permanent marker across the plastic. All these years, all this growth, acceptance, and Bravo-lebrity later, the guy with Perso-Arabic hand tattoos can't handle two syllables? I'm right here in front of you, homie. If you aren't sure, take two seconds to ask, and never mess it up again. I'm seriously in here every day!

Looking back, I wish I could give my younger self this advice: You may not see yourself reflected in your surroundings, but it doesn't mean you're not welcome there. If there is one eternal truth of humanity, it's that the need of the individual to define his or herself will always be fighting against society's effort to assimilate you. This is particularly true for outsiders looking to make their way in a strange, new world. That's what Beverly Hills was to me as a kid. *Strange. New.* And suddenly and unexpectedly, it was my world.

So, what do you do if you find yourself surrounded by people who have no understanding of what it really means to be you? People who make all kinds of assumptions about you based on the way you look or the country you are from instead of getting to know who you are as an individual? You know, the stuff that really matters: your values, dreams, history, emotional makeup, and taste in Rolex. What I've done is figure it out as I go. I sure as hell didn't always get it right and never had a map for where I was headed. At times, I've had no idea how the little strokes from one week to the next would create ripples and waves capable of upsetting and reshaping an ocean of attitudes and perceptions, starting with my own.

For me, the past forty years—*okay*, fifty years—have been a journey of realizing I'm worthy of my surroundings, and you best *believe* I belong anywhere I want to be. I didn't have a lane when I started, but I've got one now. And I'm cruising along, wind in my hair, shades on point, in a drop-top special-edition Benz.

I'm amazing. Everything about me—including where I came from—is amazing. I use the past tense because Iran was still an incredible place when I left. The Ayatollah isn't what being Persian means to me in the slightest. I don't rep that worthless tyrant. No self-respecting Persian I know does. If you don't understand what I'm talking about, thank you for reading my book because, my friend, you're about to find out what it truly means to be Persian—just like I had to.

Remember, I was four years old when I left Iran. I still have vivid, positive memories of my first neighborhood and my first house. But at that age, it's not tied to anything you can articulate in terms of culture, country, or identity. It was home, nothing more. It carried the smells and tastes of home. It was fresh-baked goods; expensive rugs; and the vibrant energy of the friends, family, and music that surrounded me. I remember Iran as warmth, happiness, safety, and fun. Imagine that—a gay man associating the Ayatollah's Iran with warmth, happiness, safety, and fun. Being gay, Jewish, and well off makes you a victim three times over in that backward place. Your boy does not make himself the victim *ever.*

Keep that in mind as you read this. I'm looking back over my life and relaying some of the negative experiences and the challenges I've faced along the way, but I'm not doing it as a means of complaint or trying to garner sympathy. Trust me, honey, that ain't me. I am not a big fan of people who try to lay blame for their failures on forces beyond their control. We all get dumped on at times, but if you make yourself out to be a poor, unfortunate soul, that's exactly how you'll end up, and I don't have time for you. Rain falls on the just and the unjust alike, sister. Deal with it and keep moving forward. Find the diamonds in the dog doodoo. I promise they are there. I've got a drawer full of them.

I'm telling you the tough parts of my story because they are the truth and because they illustrate how I have always made a conscious effort to find the good in everything. I do that to this day. If you ask me, "Did you have an amazing life, or did you have a crappy life?" I would be totally remiss if I didn't point out all the fabulous things I've gotten to do. Honestly, everything I've ever wanted to do, I've gotten to do. But imagine how boring my story would be if it was all sunshine, rainbows, and rainbow flags at the pride parade. I regard strife not as an excuse but as a badge of honor. I didn't *have* to face challenges. I was *privileged* to face challenges. If they hadn't been there, I'd never be able to say I overcame them or that I found the good in them. I get to say both with my chin up and head held high. I encourage you to approach the challenges in your own life with that attitude. It has served me well.

Having said that, the thing I spent the longest time trying to find the good in was the place I was born. The journey to appreciate that place was one hell of an expensive and time-consuming boulder to haul up a hill. I've spent a small fortune on keepsakes and relics of that precious pre-theocratic, dare I say, golden age. Why? Because that place is the ninth circle of hell, right? It's a terrible place. It's a dangerous place. It's an oppressive place. However, I am *of* that place. It's associated with me whether I like it or not. I had no choice but to dig into the history and extract the things from there I want to be associated with. This was for my own sake, and now it is for yours. Want to associate Persians with something? Here it is:

The modern Ayatollah's Iran (say it with me: "ee-RON")

does not resemble the Shah's Iran I was born to in any way, shape, or form. The Shah's Iran was progressive, opulent, glamorous, and promoting of an open and inclusive society. The Shah himself was grand. He wore a huge crown and a cape. A real-life man in a cape? He was Superman to me! He was dripping in gold and jewels, too. He carried a scepter. Who in the early seventies was walking around carrying a gold, jewel-encrusted scepter? The Shah and the royal family of Iran were my earliest idea of what it meant to achieve affluence or something special in life. The wealth being flaunted was not something to abhor, like so many of the Ayatollah's supporters thought. It was something to aspire to. A source of drive and ambition. A goal to be achieved. I would see the Shah on television with all the pomp and wardrobe and ritual circumstance and think, *That's who I want to be when I grow up! I want to be a damn shah!*

But I'm not some queen who wanted to wear a cape and a crown when he was a kid. The shah I idolized was beyond a showpiece. He was truly powerful. He was articulate and smart. He spoke multiple languages and traveled the world. He had a spine. He was not a political pawn; he was a warrior for his values. He didn't bend to his surroundings; he shaped them. He was all about prosperity. He wanted to lift people up. *All people.* Not stamp them down.

He wasn't the ruthless, mean, black-cowled old man with

a scary white wizard's beard you see lording over that country today. Mohammad Reza Shah was taking Iran away from theocracy and fanaticism. He was continuing the work of his predecessor, Reza Shah the Great, Mohammad Reza's father and the founder of the last dynasty. During *his* reign, Reza Shah had banned women from wearing the chador (a full-body length covering) and the veil in public. He wanted Persians to adopt European dress as a means of promoting a national identity for Iran, thus eliminating conflicts arising from tribal, regional, religious, and class-based attitudes. Reza Shah took his wife and daughters out in the streets in Western dress. They were living what they preached, really urging the country into a more relaxed, secular direction. Freedom of and from religion sound familiar? How about individual liberty? That was the Shah's goal for Iran.

Unfortunately, even as this wave of change was rolling through, there were still a lot of religious zealots in Iran. These fundamentalists didn't want a Western culture. They scoffed at the idea of women exposing the shape of their bodies, faces, or even their hair. They didn't like that women were encouraged to attend school and could mix freely with men. They especially hated rock 'n' roll music, and here the Shah was giving rise to a culture that produced a sexy and free-spoken female singer named Googoosh. (She's now known as the Persian Madonna, but she was Madonna *before* Madonna, in the sixties and seventies.) That is all to say, shit was changing way too fast for many who knew nothing of the world but what they learned from the Koran and an imam. The horrifying truth is, those people would ultimately win the day, and Mohammad Reza Shah would not see it coming soon enough to do anything about it.

How did he not see it coming? The more I've studied and learned about the history of the Shah, the more that question has bugged me. Why wasn't there someone to tell him, "Yo, this shit is about to hit the fan. There's a revolution popping off! Do something to stop it!" It didn't spontaneously happen. He had control of the country and the military. Why did he sit there like a frog in warm water, not hopping out until it was hot enough to cook his ass? Why didn't he start blasting fools and end the uprising when it first started? How did he lose our whole country? I think I now understand a part of it.

It's often the case that the richest, most powerful people get both the best and the worst service. Look at Princess Diana, Prince, and even Michael Jackson. People told them what they *wanted* to hear, not what they *needed* to hear. People would drop to their knees and kiss Mohammad Reza Shah's feet, but they wouldn't tell him the truth. Even up to the last moment. Things were so hairy when he left the palace for the last time that he and the queen took separate helicopters. If one was shot down on the way to the airport, there would be a living parent for their four children. But even with that level of precaution, that day the Shah did not realize he'd never set foot in his palace again. Homeboy had to flee once before, but he came back. So, this time, as he was heading to the plane, he didn't know why people were dropping status and kissing his feet as he was walking away. He thought it was precautionary, not that the monarchy was about to be dissolved and his ideas of what a modern Iran could be and what it meant to be Persian would dissolve with it. Imagine your life on a computer hard drive filled with decades of history, photographs, culture, ideas, humor, music, art, journals, memories, and recipes, and it was all wiped out, reduced to a blinking cursor and there's a madman at the keyboard. That's what happened to Iran.

You have to understand, this understanding came to me in retrospect. Like I said, I've spent a lifetime hunting down relics and keepsakes, mementos and stories from this fallen kingdom in an effort to understand it so I could be a real champion for preserving it. I've not only read every book, I've collected them. I'm a regular at auctions and events. If Mohammad Reza Shah and his royal lineage and legacy are in play, I'm there. I've spent thousands of dollars on pieces of the Shah's dinnerware, gold coins of the realm, stacks of out-of-print books, and everything in between. I've purchased and read books written by everyone from the Shah's first, second, and third wives (homie was a player) to his valet. Seriously, his valet wrote a book, and it's full of all the mundane shit Mohammad Reza would do every day. I read it and I loved it. I wanted to know everything. How can I emulate him if I don't know the details of his day? *How many minutes did he spend brushing his teeth?* I'll set a timer on my Daytona and persist as he did till the grill is pearly, get me?

He had a twin sister who wrote a book called *Faces in a Mirror*, which is out of print. You better believe I paid hundreds for that one alone. I dug and dug to get to the bottom of *how he got caught off guard.* Having that happen to me became my greatest fear. To this day, I never want to let my guard down. That was the Shah's Achilles' heel. How do I avoid it?

By being vigilant as hell.

It was an exhaustive self-education into what I love about being Persian. What does it mean to be Persian rather than Iranian? Iran is a place. Persian is a culture and a way of being. It's an attitude and a state of mind. Today, in my eyes, being Persian means being from a time and place that no longer exists. So much of the beauty that once was is still alive where I live in the United States, in the people and communities that still honor that time and place.

CHAPTER 2

MY PERMANENT VACATION

The first domino fell when my mother's youngest sister decided to move to Beverly Hills with her husband. My mom, mostly interested in escaping the incoming desert heat in Tehran, figured we'd all go. We could help my khaleh (aunt) and amoo (uncle) get settled in their new home, and we'd make a vacation out of it. The Shah was still in power at this time, and there were rumblings of danger—political discord sown by fanatics. But the idea that this ideological upheaval would somehow capsize so glorious and steady a ship was unthinkable.

So, my mom, dad, older sister, and I followed along without worry—four suitcases full of fresh threads in tow. My mother taught me that whenever you travel, you need to get new clothes to take with you. It was something of a contradiction, because she also taught me that you don't buy clothes when you're under the gun and need them. You buy them regularly, so you always have them on hand. If a Lacoste shirt looks good on you in red, it'll probably look good on you in every other color, so you should buy them all now (because who knows when you might need them). Traveling is the exception. You need special clothes for vacation, so you buy them before you go. New experiences call for new gear. With that and nothing more, we unwittingly boarded the last flight out of Iran we would ever take. The old faves, the staples, were left behind in lieu of the new stuff we brought to Beverly Hills, which would soon become the only possessions we had to our name in this world.

Globe-trotting as a family was not new to us. Dad had a successful rug business back in Tehran, and it more than afforded us a degree of luxury. This was, however, my first turn in Southern California. I remember how small Beverly Hills felt to me compared to Tehran. In all of Los Angeles, there are about half the number of people as there are in Tehran—a city closer in size and feel to New York City. The population is condensed there, too, whereas everything in Los Angeles is spread out. In LA, you have to drive anywhere you want to go. I remember thinking we were spending a lot of time in the car and not getting anywhere. Turns out, that's exactly what we were doing. I still do that. That's living in Los Angeles.

We were having a great time staying with my aunt and uncle in their new—albeit modest by comparison to ours—home. We spent our time exploring all the fantastic and glamorous offerings Los Angeles and the broader Southern California environment had to offer.

After a few weeks of playing in the warm California sun and enjoying all the trappings, tensions in Iran were escalating into violence and turning deadly. We got spooked (rightfully so) and decided to extend our two-month vacation—a move we were lucky enough to have the financial means to do. When we first made the decision to stay in the United States a little longer, we did so with the expectation that things in Iran would blow over. Then these little moments of, "Let's give it a couple of more weeks," started stacking up, one on top of the other. We would call my aunt Khaleh Nahid, the oldest sister living in Iran, frequently for updates, just waiting for her to give us the blessing to come back, but things kept getting worse and worse. Prime ministers were changing. Banks were going on strike. The garbage wasn't getting picked up. She kept telling us that, until things calm down, we'd be better off chilling abroad. So, we did. We took vacations from our vacation, traveling to places like Hawaii and Mexico while we waited for the calm after the storm. But the calm never came. Like so many other Persian families, when we saw our country turn into a place of terror and oppression, returning home became an impossibility. There was no home to return to.

Look around your house. Seriously take a second and look around. Can you imagine walking away from it all, thinking you'd be coming back after a week in Tokyo only to find out later you'd never see any of it again? Surprise! Tokyo is your new full-time spot. You're an unemployed refugee. If you want to eat, you better learn Japanese, stat. The most fly gear in your closet, gifts and other sentimental things, your hot neighbor, your ten-step skincare routine—it's all being left behind. You're leaving everything except whatever you fit into one tiny Tumi bag. Sometimes thinking back on this shit stresses me out more now than it did then. I need two bags *minimum* for a weekend in Palm Springs.

But that's how it was for us. One minute we owned a nice house and a successful business in Tehran, the next we're terrified our green cards will get revoked for some indiscretion and our desire to become instant Americans will end with a one-way trip back to face a hangman's noose. If you think I'm exaggerating for effect, I'm not. That fear was entirely literal and real. We watched our country on television from Beverly Hills, horrified, like the rest of the Western world, when the Ayatollah Khomeini took power and started hanging people from cranes. People like my parents. My mom was Muslim, yeah, but she was a rebel. She married outside her religion, which was unheard of at the time. My dad was Jewish. He'd be dead for no other reason than being Jewish, let alone marrying a Muslim woman. These two should not have been together according to their respective religions. Meanwhile, my beautiful mother's baseline joie de vivre was grounds for execution under the new regime. My folks were outwardly rich, and I liked when they would show it off. There were posed pictures of us all over our house looking like the royal family. My mom was going to Rome and Venice in the sixties buying Versace then coming back and preening for pics sprawled on the hood of my dad's Mercedes. Everything about my mom screamed *hell yes*, but marrying a Jew and showing off your looks and wealth became a death sentence under this regime.

We lost all the tangible stuff. Our home. And we also lost our community. The family business. But there was so much more to this. It wasn't like a flood or natural disaster, where you can collect the insurance and rebuild. We lost our history. We lost what it meant to be us. We lost our fundamental beliefs about what was and was not a proper society. The air we breathed and the very ground beneath our feet was swept away. That place of belonging, the name Reza on a tiny license plate? Vanished. It was heartbreaking to see it unfold, like watching a documentary that you were unwillingly the subject of. You sit and watch hoping for the best possible outcome, but the ending sucks. Many years later, I was on a flight—American Airlines appropriately—when I first saw the movie *Argo*, and all those emotions came flooding back. I watched that movie in tears in first class, and even though I knew it was a movie, I kept hoping the ending would change. That beautiful Ben Affleck would make it so the Shah returned to power and the Ayatollah was defeated. But that would be fiction. There was no Hollywood ending. The down ending is historical fact.

As it happened, along with all the other tumbling institutions in Iran, the banks were seized and accounts were frozen. Much of my family's wealth evaporated in an instant. My dad started hustling hard. Here's a guy who had to hit reset in his thirties with a family to support in a foreign country with not a whole hell of a lot to kick off of. As consummate a businessman as my father was, who was going to do business with him in Beverly Hills? My family and I might have been the oppositional force when it came to what was going on in Iran, but oddly it didn't make us allies among Americans. All most Americans knew about Iran, and Persians by proxy, was what they saw on TV. And at that time, what they saw was that a group of Persians had the gall to invade the U.S. embassy in Tehran.

It had been a while since a political or global event riled up that American sense of collective defense, but here it was in full swing. A group of Persians had broken into the U.S. embassy, technically an invasion of U.S. soil, and were holding innocent Americans hostage.

We were all guilty in their eyes.

Today we have social media. During recent global conflicts, we could see that there were citizens in Russia who did not support their own country's invasion of Ukraine. We could hear their stories and perspectives and know that people of certain nationalities or ethnicities are not a monolith. But we didn't have that kind of exposure in the seventies. We weren't subject to internment camps like the Japanese in World War II, but even at that time in California, we were the enemy. Random people in the street would scream at us, "Go back to your country!" What do you say back to that? *We don't have a country anymore! We love it here! Thanks?* It wasn't only Americans, either. My mom was once called a "terrorista" on one of our trips. They even hated us in Mexico. And why not? Walter Cronkite was there every fucking night for 444 days straight during the hostage crisis making sure everyone knew how terrified Americans needed to be. He would talk about the American hostages. They would show Khomeini, an angry, menacing old man who wanted the Shah brought back and killed. The Shah. My idol. Hung from a crane in prime time. That's what Khomeini wanted. It was horrendous.

I turned five in America while all this was happening. Think about all those little experiences you take for granted, simply because they're habits. Think about the creature comforts that made you *feel* at home when you were a kid, and then imagine that those, along with everything else, are taken away from you. If you're an adult and you've lived abroad for any amount of time, you've probably experienced this. You walk into a restaurant and have to ask for clarification on the menu. Everything is a little uncomfortable, a little unfamiliar, a little off. But for me at the time, this went way beyond ordering the cheese you like in your French fondue. Going to the grocery store, turning on the television, even recognizing your neighbors were no longer the source of comfort they once were. And worse, at times, they were now sources of stress.

It might sound melodramatic, but it's a fact that brand names are comforting. This is especially true for a kid. I didn't have any idea who Cap'n Crunch was, but he didn't look like he should be handling my breakfast needs. And neither did Toucan Sam, Tony the Tiger, or Count Chocula. What kind of a rogue's gallery of kiddie cuisine was this? Unfamiliarity didn't stop at the cereal aisle, either. They didn't have my milk, my juice, my yogurt... And forget about going to the neighborhood bakery for the cookies I loved. Learn to love a different cookie, kiddo. You'll never have those again. *What the hell is an Oreo?*

Television was the same thing. A stoned hippie and a talking dog fighting ghosts and monsters was not my idea of fun (at the time). They weren't my people. I'd never front on Shag and Scoob at this point, but at the time it was totally out of left field. I do remember discovering *The Flintstones*, though. I remember watching *The Pebbles and Bamm-Bamm Show* (*The Flintstones* spin-off for the uninitiated) and identifying with Schleprock of all characters. It wasn't the Yiddish-inspired name. He was all decked out in gray and perpetually gloomy. Everywhere he went a dark cloud followed him around. They called him "Bad Luck Schleprock." That's how I felt. Like I was so droopy my clothes were dragging on the ground, even though they weren't. I also started wetting my bed around this time. I didn't know why, and I couldn't figure it out; all I knew was that it made me feel horrible. I was a big boy in my mind, so why was I suddenly wetting the bed? It wasn't until many years later that I would reconcile this, when my sister was studying psychology at USC. She had the *DSM-III* (*Diagnostic and Statistical Manual of Mental Disorders*), and within its pages, it listed bed wetting as a result of childhood trauma. This gave me a retroactive get-out-of-jail-free card, some much-needed self-sympathy, for why I was wetting the bed all those years. I got to look back at that kid who was me and forgive him for that thing I always felt ashamed of.

As much as being in this new strange place was stressing me out, going back home had become a nightmare for me, E.T. be damned. When I say nightmare, I mean an actual one. I literally started to have these vivid tormenting visions in my sleep that somehow, I'd ended up back in Iran and I wouldn't know how I got there. When I started going to preschool, I was shocked to learn there was a nap time. I'm like, "Are you fucking crazy?" (Yes, I cursed at five years old.) "There's a full-on war happening and you want to take a *nap*?" I did not want to lie down and close my eyes on a cot in the middle of a room. I pushed my shit up against the wall so I could keep an eye on everything. I couldn't figure out why I was the only one who felt like this. Was I the only kid skipping *Sesame Street* at the end of the day to see what terrible things the old man with the white beard had done? How were these other kids not freaked out about what was going on? Were they totally unaware? Well, turns out I *was* the only one missing *Mr. Rogers* to watch the Ayatollah, and it was not a beautiful day in my neighborhood anymore. Everyone else in class was humming about their normal business. I was having panic attacks. I think I still have post-traumatic stress disorder

(PTSD) from growing up worrying that somehow I would end up back over there.

This pervasive anxiety and terror wasn't something that came and went like the explosion of a bomb. It lurked around every corner, echoing throughout my childhood. Even as I got a little older, I couldn't go for a bike ride in front of our house. If I was two minutes late coming inside, my mom would get in the car to start searching the streets for my ass. And for good reason—there were plenty of supporters of the Ayatollah living in America. They were bringing the revolution to our doorstep, throwing Molotov cocktails at the Shah's sister's house a few blocks over. I had no freedom, no safety, no independence. At a time when all the other kids would leave the house at dawn and come back at dusk, I was accounted for every minute of every day.

A few years after moving to California, when I was about nine, I'd gotten this gorgeous Diamondback bicycle as a gift. All I wanted to do in the world was ride that bike to school, so I begged and begged for months until my parents finally caved. I had the whole trip planned out in my mind—I even knew where I'd lock my bike up at school before I arrived. I had fancy cushioned pads (expensive ones) covering the handlebars and the frame. I didn't want those to get stolen, either, so after I locked the bike up, I was going to remove those and put them into my backpack so I could keep them on me all day. This was a serious operation I had planned. When my parents finally relented, I was so proud and excited.

I was on my bike riding through Beverly Hills feeling like the biggest shot on the block. I was Mister Independent with a cool breeze on my face and a smile in the morning sun. Until I spotted this sinister Mercedes S Class trailing my ass. A silver 450 SEL with cigarette smoke billowing from the sunroof and Persian music chugging out of the windows. Thankfully, it wasn't a death squad. My dad was following me to school to make sure nothing happened. God forbid the wrong person spots this cute little Persian kid tooling around on a fancy Diamondback unattended. There's no telling what someone might do to me. I was so pissed off, when I got to school the whole plan went out the window. I dumped my bike on the grass. Left my fancy handlebar pads, not bothering to lock it up or protect it in any way. I ran into the school, hot headed, full of steam. My dad collected the bike and threw it into the trunk. So much for that.

In that way, Beverly Hills life felt like a war zone to me. A ritzy place where shit could explode at any minute. There I was trying to gain a little independence, vying to grow up, but the world was holding me back. I was changing, wanting to trust my surroundings, but the environment was not having it.

All I would hear from the TV was, "Marg bar Shah" (death

to the Shah) at a time when I wanted to *be* the Shah and "Marg bar Amreeka" (death to America) when I was trying to *live* as an American. (Yes, by the way, I can say "America" without pronouncing it Amreeka. See, it can be done.) When Americans heard that same rhetoric, they associated me with all that hate. I wasn't yet American, but I definitely was not the person I saw on TV. So, what was I? Who was I? I was the person the Ayatollah wanted to kill for being too American. I was the person Americans didn't trust, because to them I was an extension of the Ayatollah. I was caught in the middle, trapped with no place to feel like I belonged. I'd be in school learning about history, but it was American history. It was a history I couldn't relate to at all: Native Americans, pilgrims, Thanksgiving. They're talking about a revolution in 1776, and I'm thinking, *What are you talking about? The revolution happened in 1979. This shit was last year!*

I was living with a profound sense of loneliness and loss. But here's the real kicker, the thing I felt this loss for (Iran), everyone around me thought it was garbage. So, my loss became even more confusing, muddling with a new sense of shame and embarrassment. It was like mourning a relative, then finding out that this person had committed unthinkable crimes even though they'd only ever been nice to me. I'm from the country everyone is pointing at and saying is evil. And physically, I looked like the people acting evil and saying all this terrible stuff on TV. Except

I hadn't done anything wrong. *I'm just a kid,* I thought. *Am I bad and evil, too?*

At times, that's how I felt. I was surrounded by mostly white kids in Beverly Hills, and, honestly, the white kids never accepted me. I didn't really have friends at school; I had teachers and classmates, but not friends. It was like that for my parents, too, because we were some of the first ones here, you know? We came unintentionally. We were pioneers of the American West, you might say. Pilgrims by chance trying to find a place to reestablish ourselves.

As the revolution went on overseas, more Persians started trickling in, but it wasn't long until the trickles turned into a tidal wave. Once Mohammad Reza was lost, it was a wrap. Nobody knew this at the time because the royal family kept it very tight to the vest, but when the revolution started, Mohammed Reza was already stricken with cancer and the clock was ticking. Seventeen months after he fled, he passed away in exile in Cairo. Any hope for a reclamation died with him.

At that point, everyone who could get out of Iran was coming to the United States—a lot of them were kids. Those kids ended up in the same school with me, where I became the honorary Persian tour guide to all things Beverly Hills and America. The teachers would leave it to me. Like, "Oh, *Reeeza* can show the rest of them around as they arrive." Which, honestly, although it was a job and title I didn't ask for, I was cool with it… And, "It's *Reh-zah*, ho."

There's power in numbers, right? As the Persian tour guide, I met every last Persian at the school, and it wasn't long before we all knew each other and developed the vibe of a displaced tribe. The worm turned, and I had a shit ton of friends. Like all the other American kids, I went to bar mitzvahs and birthday parties, they were just all for Persians. We segregated ourselves. It was partially to create a certain degree of comfort, but it was also a circling-of-the-wagons, strength-in-numbers kind of deal. Our grocer was Persian. Our doctors were Persian. To this day, there's a massive Persian presence in Beverly Hills and the adjacent neighborhood of Westwood, where UCLA is located. It all stems from this time.

We stuck together then because we had to, and we still do to this day. There's something of a Persian bubble in that area, and we all find comfort in it. Obviously, I married a white dude and have plenty of friends of other ethnicities now, but it was a while before I opened up to that change. In truth, I didn't have a non-Persian friend until I went to college. It went the same for my parents, too. As the Persian population increased, so did their circle. They were getting back to somewhat of a normalcy. They had more friends, so they were entertaining again and going out more and rekindling that social life they loved. Not sitting at home, glued to the terror on the television.

A lot of the friends they made and how popular they were as a couple was borne out of my dad's business. He was masterful in reestablishing himself here, but also in helping other Persian families rebuild their wealth and their lives in this country. My dad was set on making sure that outside our four walls, in the broader community and in the homes of others, the opportunity to persevere would be there. He was a remarkable guy by all accounts, but far from perfect as a human being. Understanding who he was and how he was, let's say it was a relationship I'd struggle with for a long time. For years, I was unsure exactly how I should feel or think about him or what place I should give him in my life and in my heart.

CHAPTER 3

RUG LIFE

One thing about Persians, particularly the ones I grew up surrounded by, is that we don't like to settle for second best. We want the best shit. We have an awareness of what the best shit is. If you can't afford the best shit, you better figure out a way to make more money. Nothing less than the best will do. My parents knew Beverly Hills was the best of the best in LA, so that's where they wanted to throw down our roots. The only problem was we had no money and no income. What my father *did* have though was a world-class knowledge of Persian rugs.

It was like a superpower. It's even in our last name. Farahan, directly translated, is a specific weave of Persian rug. So maybe it was genetic, if you believe talents or traits can be passed down through generations. Somewhere down the line, someone in our family must have *earned* the name Farahan. If so, my dad inherited and owned those talents. Not in making rugs mind you, but in buying and selling them. He had a sixth sense for Persian rugs. He could look at a Persian rug and see ghosts. He could pick up someone's cast-off at a garage sale in Pasadena, take one look at it and know what region of Iran it was from and in what years it was produced. Certain dyes are from certain places so he could see region in tone. And those dyes have different values. So, dyes equal dollars. But my dad could look at the thing and know exactly which dyes were used, how those dyes were produced and where. If it had a pigment alteration done to it afterward, he knew that, too.

Think of it like shopping for diamonds. There are color grades and clarity grades. D, E, and F are all colorless, but D is the highest quality color grade, and it's extremely rare. Then it goes G, H, I, J, and other grades I don't mess with. (Nothing less than the best, remember?) Then you look at the clarity scale, which ranges from visible inclusions to flawless, and again, the higher quality grades are even more rare. It's the same thing with rugs, except the rugs are crafted by people.

Dad also knew how many people were involved in making each piece. If someone had died in the course of making a Persian rug and had to be replaced by someone else who finished the job, he knew where they took over. Knowing all of that, he knew how much a Persian rug was worth just by looking at it. More importantly than that, he knew if the person selling that Persian rug *didn't* know how much it was worth.

How much could a rug be worth, you ask? Something you toss on the floor and tromp all over? Isn't knowing that value like knowing how much a vintage 1985 Adam Bomb Garbage Pail Kids card is worth? No. Persian rugs are not like any other rug in the world. They aren't mass-produced in factories and sold at Bed Bath & Beyond (God rest their souls). Persian rugs are works of art. Think not a replica poster of the ceiling of the Sistine Chapel, but the actual ceiling itself. They were commissioned, like that ceiling was. The best artisans would be given large sums of money by powerful people to create signature works for their palaces and collections. Going back centuries, to the first international trade markets, everyone always knew that the best rugs came from Persia. Kings and queens from all over the world would acquire these exquisite, prized rugs.

Through time and circumstance, many of these incredible one-of-a-kind works of art have become lost and unappreciated. Imagine someone's grandfather or father, an American fighting overseas, who came across a rug in the middle of World War II and thought it looked nice. It was light enough to lug back to the base, so he threw it into a duffle, rolled it out in the barracks, and then at the end of the tour, brought it home. That rug is a one-of-a-kind piece of art, handcrafted by two generations of villagers. (Yes, some of these rugs can take years to complete.) Then, two or three generations of owners pass it down the line before eventually leaving it to a colony of spiders in a basement somewhere in West Virginia. Years later, imagine that you decide to empty out the basement and see what you can get for all the old crap in there. So, you take out an ad in the *PennySaver*—a popular magazine back in the seventies—and list a "Persian Rug" among the treasures in your lot. One day, you get a call from a man in Beverly Hills who says he's sending you a self-addressed stamped envelope, and he wants you to send him some photographs of your Persian rug.

That's how my dad rebuilt his wealth in this country. Knowing this lost fortune was out there, my dad scoured the United States looking for people who didn't know their dusty heirloom was the most valuable thing they owned. Dad would scour *Penny Savers*, putting his own ads in them all across America, letting people know he was looking to purchase Persian rugs. If it wasn't my dad reaching out, it would be people responding to my dad's ad, saying they had a Persian rug. He would send them that self-addressed, stamped envelope, so they could send him photos. My dad was eBay way before eBay existed. If he saw a photo of a rug he wanted to examine up close, he and I would take a road trip. Some of these were drawn-out cross-country drives.

Daylight hours we'd listen to the news. After 5:00 p.m., we'd listen to cassette tapes of Persian music. We'd take with us an armed security guard and a big bag of cash. Those trips with my dad were extremely formative for me. That was when I started to see my dad not as a rug salesman, but as the thug-ass, high-end art dealer he really was.

There are knock-offs of everything: Chanel, Rolex, Nike. There are even knock-offs of the *Mona Lisa*. And there are a million knock-offs of Persian rugs, too. Like I said, my dad knew how to discern the real shit, but he usually needed to see it up close in order to do it. We didn't always strike oil. But when we did, my dad made it fucking rain till it blacked out the sky.

I remember one time we went to this house in Lexington, Kentucky. An older lady answered the door. She thought she was a boss bitch, very aggressive from the get. She said, "Mr. Farahan, I told you before you came it was five thousand. It's still five thousand. I'm not taking a penny less. Don't try to color me stupid sayin' it's not in good enough condition. Five. Thousand. Dollars." And my dad, who's usually super aggressive himself, not to mention hotheaded when someone comes at him, says without flinching, "You want five thousand? Okay."

Imagine my face, jaw on the Kentucky bluegrass, as my dad returns to the car to count the money out with the bodyguard. Excuse me, *WHAT?* I'm thinking, *who is this pushover loser and where did my real dad go? You're going to let this ancient wheezer who can't stand up straight steamroll you?* That's what was going through my head, but God forbid it came out of my mouth. I knew better than to say anything during the transaction, so I kept my shock and disappointment to myself. I looked on as my dad and the bodyguard paid this woman her five thousand dollars before rolling up the rug and returning to the car. As soon as we were out of earshot from that lady, I laid into it. "Dad, you didn't even negotiate with her? What were you doing? She says five thousand dollars and you just give it to her?" With a Cheshire cat's grin, he answers, "Son, that's an antique Heriz Serapi. It belongs in a museum. It's worth at least a quarter of a million dollars."

Me being the dumb kid, not yet schooled in how shit works, I said, "If that's the case, why didn't you give her more money for it?"

"She asked for five thousand. I gave her five thousand."

And that was that. That's how it was with us for a while, my dad and I. One road trip at a time, he rebuilt inventory, his business, and our wealth in America.

The manner in which he tracked every penny always stuck with me. Again, that attention to detail was not reserved for just one thing; it applied to *everything*. My dad used to keep a binder full of checks with him—the kind they still give you at the bank when you open an account. He took that binder everywhere. That's where he organized his finances and balanced his checkbook. Everything my dad did had a system. When he paid a bill, he would write the check number down and stamp it. And 100 percent of the time, every letter, number, or smudge he made in that binder was made in blue ink. Don't ask me why. My dad had a thing for blue ink. Maybe it was the uniformity; he started with blue, so he got stuck with it. Maybe he thought black ink was unlucky. Maybe he preferred the color blue to an obscene degree. To this day, I don't know why he only used blue ink. One time when he was on a trip—this is when I was grown, many years later in life—he left his binder behind and asked me to pay a few bills for him while he was gone. I did, and I used a black-ink pen to note it all in the binder, because I cannot resist a good prank, and I needed to know how he'd react. He. Lost. His. SHIT. To the point where I could not stop laughing, but I forced myself to in order to preserve my own life. Mel Brooks has a famous quote: "Tragedy is when I cut my finger. Comedy is when you fall into an open sewer and die." Let's say, I agree with Mel. I cannot get enough prank humor in my life. For the record, I keep my books using the same system my dad did. I only use blue ink, I write the check number down on the bill, and

I keep my business checkbook with me all the time. Except my checkbook cover isn't Wells Fargo; it's Louis Vuitton.

My dad wasn't some crazy, obsessive overlord. Far from it. He was just very particular about the details. He was in his thirties when we left Iran and our world turned upside down; he'd already fought and clawed his way to success, and suddenly, it was stripped away. Old dawg needed to learn some new tricks in a pinch. His midlife crisis was brought on by a freaking revolution, you know what I mean? Rebuilding his success was an act of defiance at that point. It was personal. That's how he saw what he was doing. It wasn't just business for him anymore. My dad was ruthless because he knew he was doing more than rebuilding his rug business for our family. If he did it right, he could build not only a business but a bridge. He could be laying the foundation for what would be a reclamation of sorts for thousands of other Persian families and for the entire endangered culture he wanted to preserve in the 90210.

Dad did it right, and in doing so, he acquired the means for so many families to rebuild here in the United States. He opened Farahan Oriental Rugs at 843 North La Cienega Boulevard in a Beverly Hills–adjacent area that is currently known as the design district. That store was a huge part of my childhood. I don't know about you, but for me, scents can spur memories or cause old feelings to resurface. The store had a distinct smell, the woodsy, rich chocolate kind you'd find in a college library. That good old-book smell. The rugs hanging and stacked in this place were works of art you could choose to either walk on or hang on a wall. They were piled high. Each one had two unique stories all its own: a story of the rug's history and a story of how my dad acquired it.

Behind the showroom, he had an office, and beyond that, way in the back, was his safe. Actually, it was more than a safe, it was a vault. The kind with a five-step combination and a huge spinning handle. It had thick cylinders running vertically and horizontally across it, and it was bolted into the concrete. That thing wasn't going anywhere, and nobody was getting into it without some serious criminal or CIA training. In that vault was a huge black plastic bag. Kind of like a Hefty trash bag. The most unassuming thing in the whole store if not the whole neighborhood. Except this bag was full of cash—hundreds of thousands of dollars in cold, hard U.S. currency, all legally gained and properly taxed. My father wasn't a criminal. He didn't need to be. But he didn't need to be purely altruistic, either. He was a shrewd businessman and someone who believed he could make a fortune by saving his countrymen and preserving the pre-revolution Iranian way of life.

At the time, people fleeing Iran for the United States couldn't bring their money with them because Iranian currency wasn't worth anything in America. On top of that, they were not allowed to bring many personal items to the States when they fled. They were having a hard time getting anything of value through customs. The one thing they *could* get through were rugs. When questioned, Persians could tell the customs agents at the airport that the rugs were prayer rugs and part of their religious practice. That was the one thing those custom agents wouldn't touch—the "prayer" rugs. They didn't want to discriminate against someone's religion, so they wouldn't even press on them. They wouldn't confiscate rugs the way they did other items. They let them bring their dusty old rugs over. So, what started happening was the Persian families would take what currency they had in Iran, go buy the most expensive rug they could afford, and bring that with them to the States. That rug was their wealth. Once they got into the States, they'd bring their rugs to my dad's showroom and exchange it for some of that cash he had in his vault.

This cash was their seed money to open a bank account. Buy a house. Start a business. Whatever they needed to get up and running in America. That's how a lot of Persian families—we're talking thousands of them—started rebuilding here. Like I mentioned before, to this day in Beverly Hills and the surrounding areas, there is still a huge Persian population, and my dad's business was a major reason for their choosing this area. Also, they were Persians, and this is Beverly Hills.

My dad saved families. He saved fortunes. He fostered a community here that allowed for the great traditions of his home country as he knew it under the Shah to be continued. Soon enough, my dad was getting his clothes pressed at the Persian dry cleaner. His shirts monogrammed at the Persian tailor. His hair done at the Persian barber. Meanwhile, I was stoked because I could get *my* milk at the Persian grocer. My favorite cookies at the Persian bakery. We could dine at Persian restaurants. And I got to play tour guide to all my new Persian friends at Beverly Vista. My world really opened up at that point, and I could imagine myself being here for the long term. I could start to see a future that made sense—one where I was around people who looked like me, sounded like me, and didn't look down on me for being different.

He may not have been a shah, but my dad was every bit the inspiration to me the image of the Shah was. Like Dad, I enjoy playing poker and gambling. I devour spicy food (the hotter the better). I consider myself a savvy businessman. Sometimes when I'm driving, I'll realize my hands are resting on the wheel and I'm holding my right middle finger just below the knuckle, with my left hand. Like he would on those long road trips while his hands rested on the wheel.

Dad built his life for success. He was an early riser, up with the roosters. He was highly motivated and almost robotic. He had a maintenance routine and he stuck to it, so he was always immaculate. His hair was always perfect. He smelled amazing, clean, and elegant to match his appearance. Never overpowering. His car, always a big S Class Mercedes or the newest Jaguar, was always detailed to the nines. Everything he wore had to be dry cleaned. His suits and monogrammed shirts were pressed. Jeans creased. And he was fit. From ages eighteen to fifty-five, his weight never changed no matter what he ate, so his genetics must have been off-the-chart fortunate. He had the looks to back all that up, too. I know how gross it is to say my dad was fine, but my dad was hot as hell back in the day. I challenge you to disagree.

As I've gotten older, I've had the opportunity to get to know a lot of my dad's family, including uncles and cousins who were around him when he was a young guy and out on the scene. Some of the stories I've heard about the lengths women would go to *be* with him are epic. Even later on, when we would go to parties and I'd be there with my mom, other women would follow my dad around the room and fawn over him. Mom found it entertaining. It was like watching a nature film. The sly lioness sneaking up on the antelope. If he was having an entertaining conversation with a group of people and he'd say something funny, you could see these hoes would laugh three, four, five times harder than they should be laughing. I'm sure that all played into his sense of self and the power he had to hold court with others, which then symbiotically fed into his focus on appearance and presence. I tend to feel claustrophobic in cars, so I always roll my window down, but when my dad and I were in the car together, he would make me roll it up. "It's blowing my head off," he'd say, palming down his thick, silver-fox-status hair, steering wheel be damned. He wasn't being mean to me. He didn't want me to suffocate. That's who he was. His hair, like everything else about his appearance, was an extension of his soul.

CHAPTER 4

THE NEEDLE TO DAD'S THREADS

My mom is absolutely amazing and nothing if not Persian to the damn bone. This bitch (and I mean that in the most adoring way) was dropped into the middle of Beverly Hills in her thirties, a product of old-school Iran, where she had social status and money, was life of the party, and was glammed out AF. Suddenly she was the new kid on the block who lived with her sister and didn't speak a word of English. She couldn't even navigate a trip to the grocery store, much less organize a party. It's hard to socialize with friends you don't have, who speak a language you don't know. Here's the thing about my mom, though; if her situation affected her negatively, she was the only person who experienced it. She never let me feel or sense any stress from her. Her energy was a positive constant through all this turmoil. She was my angel, a polestar, and she went shining through. She did her best to recreate Iran within our home one herb and one spice at a time. Then as my dad's business took off and as more Persians moved into the neighborhood, slowly but surely, the world evolved around her and allowed her to extend the shield she'd built around me in a way. She remained who she was then and now, barely missing a step. In all the best ways and some quirky ones.

She turned our home into a time capsule. From the outside, our house was nothing out of the ordinary, just everyday seventies 90210 aesthetic. Stepping inside, however, you crossed a threshold into a living museum—out of time and place into a romanticized version of what my mom thought of as Iran. All the sights, sounds, and scents, the good feelings and optimism for the future were preserved. It was like if you went to the Natural History Museum and studied remnants left behind by the Romans or the Greeks. Except here it was contemporary, from a culture lost not centuries ago but last week. Although the furniture in the new house was local to the States—pieces by Henredon, Glabman, and Mastercraft—there were Persian rugs covering every square inch of the peg-and-groove hardwood flooring.

Preserving our language was big for my mom, too. She wanted all of us to speak Farsi at home, and she wanted to make sure I grew up knowing how to speak it well. This worked for me. I'm fully bilingual. It's funny though, because she's been here the same amount of time as I have, and her English still sounds like she got here yesterday.

So much of what I've come to love about what it means to be Persian, I gleaned from my mom. She taught me a sense of abundance about our culture. If you ask my sister if we were rich when we were growing up, she might say no because there were a lot of people who were wealthier than us. I would say we were rich because we lived better than people who had more money than us, thanks to my mom. As I was coming of age, company was a constant. It was on a level that I can't explain unless you've been to a Persian wedding. There was always abundant food in our house—at least enough to feed a group of forty or so—in case a party broke out. But party or not, she always made sure we ate well. Food was a big deal to my mom. Beyond the quality and quantity, the presentation mattered equally. She wanted people to walk into our house and feel more at home there than they did in their own homes.

That's my mom's energy when it comes to her friends and family. Now multiply the Farahan guest experience by a factor of ten, and that's what childhood was like for *me*. I grew up knowing my mom—who had this rich sense of living—was obsessed with me. She told me when I came into their life that everything changed for the better. They were doing well before, but as soon as I touched down shit blew up. She said I was a lucky flower in their garden, and I perked everything up like a daisy. She matched her words with her care for me. Whatever I wanted, I feel like I got it. She showered me with kisses, hugs, support, and encouragement. I may not have been spoiled by my circumstances, but I was spoiled by my mom. It wasn't restricted to physical affection, either. From the latest in toys to the freshest of clothes to the food on my plate, I got what I needed from her. And I was equally obsessed with my mom. She was and is the most loving creature on the planet. She expressed little bits of love all around me, all the time. It was all in the details. For example, I love romaine hearts. Always have. And in 1973 the cute little bags we have today containing only the hearts of romaine lettuce didn't exist. Tough times, for sure. Ever since I can remember, my mom would get four extra heads of lettuce at the store so there'd be a special side of salad for me at the table, containing only the best part of the salad—in my opinion, the hearts. To me, that's love. That extra step of making sure I had something special. It's the type of consideration I try to give to my loved ones. Carrying on her legacy in this way is important to me.

Food has always been a part of my love language, in good ways and in bad. I don't know if my mom fed into that, or if I was born that way and she recognized and nourished it. Like most things, I suppose it's a bit of both. If you come to my house, even for a casual get-together, I will have a smorgasbord of offerings to express how much I care about you and your presence. I'm not talking about day-old bread and cheese slices, either. My mom didn't know what a fish stick was and neither do I. As my guest, you'll be treated to precisely cut fresh fruit, high-quality cold cuts, mint in your ice cubes, mother-of-pearl spoons in the caviar, and fresh flowers always. My mom didn't mess with plastic plants. They have no scent. There's no experience to be had with them, and we are all about the experience. Love in all forms is a fabulous vibe. I aim to own that vibe the way my mom did.

Food has been a negative at times, too. Early in my life when I was lacking confidence, uncertain about my sexuality and how it would be received, I hid behind calories. Later, when I was searching for love or in need of feeling loved, I did the same. All you have to do to know what was going on with my emotional health at any point in time in my life is track my weight. I carried misery in my midsection. In more recent years as I've learned to love myself more and put more energy into my loving relationships, I don't lean on food in the same way I once did. I do continue to show up for others through food, though.

Another thing I get in large part from my mom is my love of jewelry. Mom wasn't into cars or handbags. She didn't want every fancy thing in the world for the sake of having it. She was into shit that sparkled. Back in the day, there was a Parisian jeweler in Beverly Hills named Fred Joaillier. Mom always wanted *something* from Fred. Dad delivered. Growing up, all the bling my mom got from Fred would end up in a safe she hid in her bedroom closet (again, my folks with the safes). It was beneath where the clothes hung, hidden by a flop of carpet. Being the sneaky observer I was—okay *am*—I knew the combination. I probably only saw her unlock the safe once, but I knew the combo from there on out. Those are the types of things I notice. If you cut your hair slightly differently, use a new plate to cover your light switch in order to conceal a chip in the paint, use a specific key to open your mail, I'm going to catch it. If you tell me a little white lie and over time your story changes, I'm going to remember both versions of the story. It's the way I operate. Ever vigilant and detail oriented. Never to be caught off guard. So anyway, I knew how to open the safe. And as soon as she'd leave the house, I'd empty that shit and spread all her amazing bling out in front of me like a treasure-happy pirate. I'd adorn myself in her necklaces, barrettes, bracelets, with a bauble on every finger. I made myself all jeweled up like the Shah. I was in my element, decorated in sparkling expensive accessories. I'd pose in the mirror like I was Shah Reza of Beverly Hills. I did it all the time. I'd anticipate her leaving and anxiously await the moment I could run upstairs and get into her getup. One time, I was standing before a mirror, admiring myself bedazzled to the nines when I heard the door to the garage shut unexpectedly. Shit! I quickly, carefully slid each piece off my neck, arms, and fingers before placing them back into the safe and reverse engineering my whole caper. I hurried downstairs, collecting my calm as I went. I mentally high-fived myself as I met my mom in the kitchen, coming in with the groceries. I'd gotten away with it. "Need a hand, Mom?" Mom was looking at me, and it wasn't her usual look of a mother's love but something less adoring. Her narrowed eyes shot daggers at the crown of my head. My hand fumbled into my hair as I met her gaze—*the diamond barrettes*! She took them off for me and started chasing my ass around the house *Tom and Jerry* style. That was the last time I ever made it into her safe, because that clever woman put a sewing needle with thread in the crease of the door, so she would know if a certain someone snuck in again. My diamond-donning days were put on pause…for a while.

For me, being Persian was personified by this incredible woman to whom I meant everything. To make sure that thread of my upbringing, so frayed by war, never broke was her endeavor. She prided herself in it. It breaks my heart to this day when I think back and realize I let my own silly childish embarrassment betray her in that.

When you look back at your childhood, it's not like you're thinking moment by moment through an entire day, or month, or year. Memories aren't movies. You don't retain everything. Most of your life is forgotten even by you. It's a humbling realization. What you retain are these clips of events and things you did and things other people did, all bound together by the senses and emotions of the moment. Some of those emotions, particularly the painful ones, never lose their potency. In fact, some cuts that never heal hurt worse when you think back because the context you give them only gets heavier as you go. This is all true of a sandwich for me. I still get teary eyed and filled with regret when I think about this one particular sandwich. My mother made it for me with so much care, this beautiful kotlet sandwich. I was in first or second grade, sitting in the back of the school cafeteria when I pulled it out of my lunch box. The bread was long and in the shape of a tic-tac. It had grooves in it. It looked like the back seat of a 1979 450 SEL with all its ridges, and it was covered in sesame seeds. Crispy on the outside and soft on the inside. In Persian sandwiches, instead of lettuce, pickles, and tomatoes, you use different herbs like tarragon, saffron, mint, and basil. The kotlet itself is a mixture of ground beef and potato that has been fried in oil. It's a food that takes true effort to make. You can smell and taste all the preparation and work that goes into creating it. In Iran, this meal was a common scent; you could always smell the mouthwatering savory ingredients when someone's mom was making this particular staple. So, I was sitting there in the cafeteria, starting to bite into this incredible meal my mother had made for me, when a group of kids assembled, interrogating me about this crazy-smelling sandwich. It didn't look like what they were used to eating. They told me how gross it looked and how funny and awful it smelled. They told me it was making the whole cafeteria stink and that if I wanted to eat it, I needed to take it outside. They made me feel so horrible, so beaten down and embarrassed about this freaking sandwich my mom made for me. My cheeks and ears started to burn hot as I grew more and more upset. I got up, took my sandwich, and threw it in the trash. I caved in. I let them make me feel disgusted by an act of love from my mom. She'd made that sandwich for me with the same hands that now shake because she's old and frail. I'd wasted her time and care. This was something she'd done, not to feed me, but to make sure that my world *wasn't* interrupted by everything going on. She wanted me to feel safe and taken care of. I let a bunch of jerky kids drive me to throw that in the garbage. For what? For whom? Nobody benefited from that choice I made. I didn't see it then, so from that day on I never brought food from home again. I wouldn't let my mom make my lunch. I would get mad at her if she tried. Instead, I bought the crappy cafeteria food like everyone else. I still carry the guilt of that every day. In a critical time, I took something so special and important away from her, and I did it for nothing. I did it for some dumbass punk kids who I let harass me. I look back at that now in tears. Like a little piece of me died that day. And it stayed dead for a long time. I gave up on being accepted at school; I didn't want to be openly harassed. So, I turned into a zombie. I was dead inside all day. Then I'd drag my feet home, up to the front door, and push myself into the foyer. As soon as the door closed behind me, I belonged again. Home was my refuge. My only safe space in the world. There, I stopped being the foreign kid with the smelly sandwich and the unpronounceable name. There I was Reza. My name always came out right. My mother was my world. She still is. And to my mother, I remain the world.

CHAPTER 5

ROMEO AND JOON-IET

I was thirteen, gazing blankly into the powder room of our house, which was undergoing a remodel. The floor had been torn out and I could see the concrete subflooring. Tiles were leaning against the wall, waiting to be installed. They were beautiful white alabaster—or maybe terrazzo with a quartz aggregate, my mind's eye is a little fuzzy—and I picked one up in both hands and carried it outside. I still remember the weight. The tile, mind you, had nothing to do with what I was about to do. I wasn't yet much of an interior design critic. I was feeling helpless, and the tile was the only thing of value more helpless at the time. I walked it down the stairs and outside, taking it into the alley behind our house and walking a couple of houses down to get out of ear shot. I lifted the tile overhead, and with everything I had, I slammed it to the ground. It shattered into pieces. The crash felt good in the moment, but that wasn't my only goal. I had hoped this release of aggression would alleviate the weight I was carrying in my chest. And when the tile smashed into the hard ground, that hope had broken and scattered across the alley along with it. Nothing had changed, in fact, but the state of the tile. I felt no better.

My parents were lucky I didn't burn the whole house down, renovation be damned. I started dreaming that the house would burn down when we were all gone. I thought if the house went down in flames, maybe our problems would disappear with it. I was attaching problems to a time and a place. So, if that place and that time didn't exist anymore, neither would the problems. All we had to do was torch the current place and move to a new place in order to move forward as a family. We could leave all the negativity and conflict behind. That's all I wanted to do. I wanted to leave. Our house wasn't home anymore. I resented it. Everything my mother had cultivated—the delicious smells and tastes, the inviting aura and essence of our Persian home—were preserved only to eventually go sour. Maybe it was always meant to be, even if it wasn't her fault.

My parents met in Tehran in the midsixties. My mother has an older sister, and that older sister had a boyfriend at the time.

He was in the military with my dad. Back then, it was taboo in Iran for an unmarried couple to go out on a date alone, so when my aunt wanted to go out with her boyfriend, my mom would go along as her chaperone and my dad would accompany the boyfriend as his plus one. And, like I told you, my dad was *so damn fine* back in the day. (I know, it's weird. But truth is truth!) He wasn't alone in his fineness, as my mother was insanely gorgeous. And in the process of chaperoning the other two, they fell in love.

Fun fact: My dad had another wife before he married my mom. It was for a very hot minute. Like a Kim Kardashian–Kris Humphries type of marriage. Short and quick. Nothing the family would remember, but it happened. Wife number one was a Muslim, too. Dad had a type evidently. At least in wives. Rebellious Muslim women were a thing for him, even though he and his family were Jewish. I'm no psychotherapist, but I think this had to do with him not having great feelings about his own Jewish mother. My dad's mom was something of a villain in my dad's life, and by proxy, mine as well. She never liked my mother, and I think you have to be mentally deranged to not like my mother. When my dad was still very young, his mother divorced his father—who loved her very, very much—basically abandoning my dad in the process. I cannot imagine a mother wanting to walk away from her children, but this ho did. So, my dad grew up without his mom. She lingered on the periphery, but she was the polar opposite of what my mom was to me.

That betrayal must have put my dad in a space where anyone resembling his own mother would have been off-putting. He wanted something else. So, he was like, "Where the goy bitches at? I'm down with them." And they were down with him, too, but that didn't mean their families were. Even though young Muslim women were undergoing something of a liberation at the time, their parents were still very traditional, and my maternal grandparents were no exception. As far as their views on a marriage between my mom and dad, my Muslim grandfather told my mom flat out she couldn't marry my dad because he was a Jew. But my mom wouldn't take no for an answer. She told my grandfather she was in love with my dad and that she wanted to be with him and only him. (In case you couldn't tell, my mother was very strong-willed.) Eventually, my grandfather relented and approved of the marriage. But not without this caveat he gave my dad: "Don't be taking her around any of those Jews, because that's not going to be okay with me." Believe it or not, my dad agreed to the terms. He really wanted to marry my mom. He didn't like his own mom, anyway, so what's a few extended relatives in exchange for the love of your life? My dad gave up a whole religion for my mother, not to mention alienated himself from his family for most of his adult life. And he stuck to his word. I didn't even know my dad was Jewish until I was eight or nine years old. It was a family secret up to that point. And to keep that secret going, there was little to no connection between my dad's family and us. So, I grew up knowing my dad had a mom, but that she wanted nothing to do with us.

My parents were 100 percent committed to each other in that way. It was the two of them against the world, ride or die, for the longest time. They defied all odds. They were perfect partners. While my dad was out building his business and taking care of everything on the financial side, my mom was at home making sure our home was a safe place for our hearts to live. Like I said, our home was always full of warmth, music, food, and affection. She wasn't some Suzy Homemaker out of a fifties sitcom, wandering around in an apron pushing a vacuum all day, though. She was once again a philanthropist and socialite in the new world, very capable of other things, but she was a wife and mother first. Somehow, she managed all of that responsibility through her hospitable and domestic nature with incredible grace. She was magic.

So, how could my dad betray her and betray us all by running around behind our backs with other women? Scratch that. He wasn't limiting himself to running around with another woman. He was throwing money at these hoes. Yes, *plural*. There were many of them, all at the same time. There were probably more than we will ever know of, in fact. He wasn't casting far to reel them in, either. He didn't have hoes in different area codes. It was the dry cleaner. It was the tailor. It was the hair stylist. I swear he had one at the car wash, too. It was the girls from the parties. They were all locals. They were all part of our circle. God forbid being a player interrupted his daily routine. One of them was an old friend, half of a couple my parents had been friends with since they lived in Iran. Their son had been in a tragic accident when he was sitting in the bed of a pickup truck and the driver broke really hard sending the kid backward, snapping his spinal cord on the lip of the tailgate. His family didn't have medical insurance at the time, so they needed a lot of help, which my dad was giving them. We all knew about it. He was helping with finances, connections, and other means of support. What we *didn't* know was that he was also being generous with the mother's sexual needs during this time. These weren't girls he was just buying simple gifts. Let me be clear about that. He was renting these women *apartments*, paying their bills, buying them shit, the whole nine. Which makes it worse than a sexual fling, in my opinion. He was supporting them the way a person supports their family. But they weren't his family. We were.

Finding out about dad's dalliances made me so damn angry. Instead of focusing on us and propping us up, he was floating these randoms? WTF? Talk about shockwaves. My bones were rattled to their core. It wasn't like a frog being dropped into boiling water, though. Discovering that my dad was cheating was a process. I told you, I'm always vigilant, always tracking details; I never want to be caught off guard. The subtleties of my dad's shifting behaviors weren't lost on me. I wasn't old enough yet to be able to suss out the "why" of it all. For instance, I was aware my mother had turned it up a notch for some reason. She was dressing up more. She was wearing more makeup. The house was cleaner. There were more fresh-cut flowers everywhere. So, I knew something was fishy. The puzzle came into focus suddenly, though, when I heard them fighting one night. It was the cliché scene you'd expect, too. Sad little Reza at the top of the stairs, curled up with his knees to his chest eavesdropping, Mom and Dad's voices carrying from somewhere downstairs, slightly muffled through a closed door. My mom basically laid it all out in that argument and then I knew. Everything was crystal clear. She had already known, of course, and was trying to make things right and bring Dad's attention back where it belonged. But it had been to no avail. Dad was never going to be the hero I saw him as ever again. He was never going to be my dad in the same way again for that matter, either. In fact, I'd been fooled by this dick. Taken by surprise. My kingdom was crumbling around me, and here I thought Mom was just feeling the need to smell better.

I was furious. So, I picked up that bathroom tile and carried it and my rage into the alley. *Boom!*

After that night, everything changed. Once I knew what my dad was doing, I no longer revered him the way I had before. I was grossed out. I remember in the wake of that fight, my folks realized I'd overheard everything and immediately went into damage control. What do you do when you want a kid to calm down? Offer him a treat. So, my mom and dad took me to the farmers' market at Beverly Grove to get some ice cream. My mom was not ready to call it a wrap with Dad, even with everything he'd done. The plan was that she was going to hold our life together, that she would get Dad to stop screwing around and make things work between them. Things were going to be like they'd always been.

As we were sitting outside, having ice cream and calming down from the explosion of tears and raised voices that had erupted, my mom asked me for a taste of my ice cream. A strawberry cheesecake cone. I remember it vividly. Of course, I let her have some. Then she told me to offer some to my dad. Mom was pushing me to forgive as fast as she apparently had. I let him taste the ice cream, even though I didn't want to. He licked my ice cream, and I was repulsed. It was like watching some unbathed, homeless stray wrap their lips around it. My dad was suddenly a grotesque stranger to me. It really turned my stomach. I didn't want to put my mouth on the same ice cream my dad had. That's how disgusted I was with him. So, I got up after he took his bite and threw the rest of it out. A treat wasn't going to fix this.

The trips to find rugs didn't stop, though. It was quite the opposite, actually. I went with him even more often, because my mom wanted me to keep an eye on him. I became her defender and protector not only in theory but in practice as well. They were trying to make it work through me, the loyal son, so I was trying to do whatever I could to make it work for them. Our road trips weren't the same, though. It seemed the Mercedes had grown in size to account for the distance I now felt from the man in the driver's seat. It became, for me, more of an obligation than an adventure. Whatever safety bubble I had left as a child—and the only one I ever had was in the security of my parents' relationship and in my home—had burst. I felt like I was in a barren wasteland where the only polestar I had left was my obligation to honor and take care of my mother. My model for what a successful romantic relationship looked like was shattered like that tile. Never mind the fact that I was starting to understand that I was way more interested in boys than I was in girls, if I had any interest in them at all. To say the world was hazy around me at that point was an understatement.

It was on one of those post-meltdown trips that I was finally introduced to my dad's family. You know, all the Jews he had essentially disowned in order to marry my mother. I don't say that dismissively of the religion. I am Jewish myself. But my connection to Judaism had been solely fostered by my dad, not through any broader affiliation with his family. Remember, marrying my mom meant my dad honoring his promise to my mother's father about not bringing her around other Jews. Now that his marriage was falling apart, my dad was reaching out to them, trying to reestablish relationships on that front. He was always planning the next move, I guess. Maybe he really missed his connection to them throughout his entire marriage. I don't know for sure, but I do know from being alive, that, generally speaking, when a husband is caught cheating on his wife, he becomes ostracized by all the shared friends and of course the in-laws. It's common for them to turn to the only people who will continue to associate with them nonjudgmentally, and that's their own family.

Anyway, Dad and I went to New York, and there they were, all these relatives I had no idea existed because my mom is Muslim. My dad had written them off so long before, they'd given up on us. Yet, here my dad is introducing me to all these cousins and aunts and uncles, and I'm like, "How the hell did I not know you existed?" I wasn't running into their arms or anything. Religious politics aside, I'm a little kid in a room full of strangers. It wasn't the warmest reception from either side.

There wasn't any of that, "Look how you've grown," or any of the normal shit that happens around family reunions. It felt like they were looking at me like I was a failed science experiment or something. This freakshow combination of a Muslim egg and Jewish sperm any God would be sure to reject. To be fair, though, that's how I felt; it's not necessarily how they thought about me. I remember feeling like they were all looking at me in a weird way when, in my mind, I was curious about them more than anything.

I was especially curious about my paternal grandmother. My dad's mom, the evil queen. It was around this time I became more conscious of her, too. Contrary to the rest of the family, who were at least willing to *glance* my way, that old bat evidently did not want to see me at all. At the time, I could not understand why. She was always in my periphery, but as an innocent kid, I didn't fully digest how bizarre that relationship was. I grew up thinking, *Okay, so my paternal grandmother lives in West LA. We live in Beverly Hills* (these are neighboring cities, if you don't know). My mom, God bless her, actually encouraged my dad to go see her once a week for lunch even though the witch hated my mom. That's my mom, though. She treats her biggest enemy with the respect she thought she deserved as a mother herself. But I never got to go to these lunches. She never called for my birthdays. Graduations. Nothing. No card with a moth-eaten five-dollar bill. Why, you ask? My grandmother didn't love me because I wasn't 100 percent Jewish. At the time, I couldn't fathom this woman. She didn't like me for reasons beyond my control. She didn't like my mother, whom I loved more than anyone. She never approved of my parents' marriage, either, the core of my family unit. Back when they were engaged, she straight up told my dad, and anyone who would listen, that my mother would make a terrible wife. As if this person should have any say or was in any way a good judge of what makes for a good wife. *Look who's talking, ho. Aren't you the same person who abandoned my grandfather and my dad when he was a young boy? Why do you think he wants to marry a Muslim in the first place?* My anger at this shadow on the wall who was supposed to be my grandmother started to grow. I didn't really know her or who she was. Was she the personification of all of my dad's worst traits? Did my mother not allow me to go to those lunches to shield me from her toxicity? She was nothing really, but suddenly she meant so much to me it turned my gut.

One day, my mom came home bawling. I could tell that she was crushed, that I was witnessing an end-of-her-rope type of despair. This was in the middle of the fallout over my dad's affairs, so there had been plenty of tears, anyway. This time, though, I could sense something was different. I asked her what was wrong. Completely distraught, she told me that she had gone to see my dad's mother, hoping to confide in her. She actually turned to this old turd in her time of need—that's how desperate she was. She pleaded with my dad's mom, "You're the matriarch of this family. My mom still lives in Iran. You are the elder. I need you to talk to your son. Talk some sense into him. He's having affairs. He's giving our money away. He's tearing apart my family." My grandmother shut my mom down. Cold ass told her, "So, what? I didn't think you should have been married in the first place. You were never right for him." She put the whole thing on my beautiful mother, who'd never so much as looked at another man while she was married to my dad. My mom had nobody on her side at that point. Except for me. And nobody fucks with my mom.

When that happened, I was hoop-earrings-out, prepared to hunt down this grandmother at her house made of candy in the woods and throw her wrinkled old ass in her own oven. I never even had so much as a letter exchange with her. But I was ready to unload a lifetime of disappointment, and I wasn't going to rest until I did. I was ready to give a "You want two cents? Here's five bucks for every birthday you missed!" type of a rant.

The only problem was I didn't know her phone number.

So, what did I do? I went full mystery machine and *Scooby Doo*'d that trick, determined to unmask her. I made it my mission to get my grandmother's phone number. It's not like I knew where she lived. Even if I found out, it's not like I could jump on my bike and peddle over or anything. I figured I didn't need her face, anyway, just her ear. I knew two places where I might be able to find her number: either my mom's or my dad's Rolodex. This is pre–cell phones and in the early days of the home computer, so I had to go full ink-and-pen. I wasn't finding that shit in the cloud. I had easy access to my mom's Rolodex. It was at the house, sitting in her bedroom. But if my grandmother's number was in there, there's no way I could have gotten it out. The whole thing was in Farsi—I could speak it, but it wasn't something I'd learned to read yet. So, it would have to be my dad's. But that was in his office at the store, which was off limits, so the whole operation took planning, timing, and me humming the *Mission Impossible* theme song to myself.

I started by telling my dad I wanted to go to work with him, which didn't draw any suspicion because I often did. Even at that age and in that situation, I was trying to glean as much as I could from my dad's business practices. After all, I might soon be the only means of support financially for myself and my mom. When we got there, I played it cool, going about my business as usual and staying out of my dad's office. I waited for my opportunity. Then while dad's secretary was out to lunch, my dad stepped away to use the bathroom, and the clock started ticking.

As soon as that office was empty, I dive-rolled behind his desk and flipped through the little cards with all the different names and numbers. The Rolodex cards were all identical. All caps, blue ink. My dad pressed down hard on that pen; another thing we have in common. You'd think he was an architect with all the letters and numbers perfectly aligned. And there it was. That cunt's information. The mortal enemy of my mother—and my mortal enemy by extension—was exposed and she didn't even know it yet. I jotted down the digits onto a scrap of paper, stuffed it into my pocket, tiptoed back to the showroom, and the stage was set.

Phase two was afoot. The next day, I waited until I was alone in the house so I could call without anyone overhearing me and interrupting or intervening on the old woman's behalf. My verbal onslaught was about to bury her, and I didn't want anyone on hand to call 911. Finally, my mom stepped out to run errands, and the showdown was on. All she had to do was answer. I grabbed the phone off the wall and punched in the numbers.

It rang, and she answered.

My first words *ever* to my own grandmother were, "You fucking bitch!" I went off. Every other word had four letters. I let it all hang out, my mouth shooting off like a Tommy gun, thinking this old woman must be heartbroken to hear her sweet grandson, whom she never knew, furiously defending his mother. I'm thinking for sure she was going into cardiac arrest and stroking out while I unloaded. It didn't take that old bitch two seconds to turn it around on me. She shouted something along the lines of, "Fuck you, motherfucker! If you ever call again, I'm gonna fucking slaughter your half-breed ass!"

She hung up on *me*!

Here I am thinking I had figured out a way to unleash all the anger and resentment I had, when in fact, I walked away feeling a thousand times worse. I got cussed out by my own grandmother. An old lady called me a motherfucker and hung up on me. Where's the pride in that?

Over the years, my parents' relationship devolved as a result of my father's hyperactive nut sack. Post-revelation, the marriage endured a good four or five years of fighting, suffering, crying, and facing each other through therapy until it was pronounced dead. The divorce and everything leading up to it was a lot of distress to deal with. One day, I came home from school (I was in high school and old enough to drive at this point) and there they were. They were sitting in what you could call the junior dining room (sorry, the real estate agent in me peaked up to say hello there). Anyway, they were yelling at each other, as had become the norm. My mom was in tears, which was also the norm at this point. I honestly don't know how someone has that many tears inside of them. You'd think the well runs dry at some point. Not when you're this sad, evidently. I made eye contact with my mom and in my head I was thinking, *I can't take this anymore. It's either him or me.* I think I managed, without a word, to communicate that to her when I turned around, slammed the door, got back in my car, and left.

That was the turning point for me in my attitude toward the whole situation. They might not have been done with their marriage, but I was. I wouldn't say my parents ever reached a turning point like I did; they were never done with their marriage. Rather, the marriage was done with them.

When my sister went off to graduate school at Chapman University in Orange County, my parents decided to downsize their living space. They rented out our house and purchased a condo in the Wilshire Corridor, which they gutted. Maybe it was the literal tearing down of walls, I'll never know for sure, but they ended it for good during the renovations. My dad never moved into the condo. My mother and I moved in when it was done, and my dad ended up moving to New York to be with the same family he once gave up to be with us. It was the end of my formative years, if you will. I didn't see my dad much after that for a long while. We were, at that point, no longer the center of his world as we had once been. He didn't abandon us completely, though, I'll give him that. He still cared and did more than his fair share to make sure I was able to launch well out of high school and get my life started on better terms than I would have been able to do on my own.

CHAPTER 6

I TOOK MY HEART TO SAN FRANCISCO

MJ knew there was something wrong. We'd been friends since high school, and by the time we graduated, we'd not only had sex twice, but we were also inseparable.

Yes, MJ and I boned.

And, yes, on more than one occasion.

If you wanted some salacious *Shah*'s tell-all fodder, there you have it. The truth is out there. Although I'm gay—and have been since I learned what sex was—I wasn't anywhere near ready to come out at that point. Also, I am hyper *hyper*sexual. I'd bang a warm breeze on a cold night if it was damp enough not to chafe. That's not to say MJ was a gust of hot air to me. Far from it. We were that close. Two purely platonic friends, so close to each other in high school that we showered together. It was during one of these friendly showers we were swapping places so I could take my turn under the water, when our bodies squeegeed between wall and window and, well, that was all it took. The shower went on longer and got a lot steamier than either of us had initially intended. Fun times with my bestie.

MJ aside, these were not so fun times for me otherwise. Days were spent watching my family unit collapse from the sideline and roaming aimlessly through the men's department at Neiman's. I lacked direction and a sense of who I had the potential to be. I was my father's son, my sister's brother, and my mother's angel. But those roles were dissolving, and therein lies the real rub. I hadn't yet figured out that life's totality is not about being who your relationships define you as. It's also about knowing who you are as an individual. Being comfortable in acting authentically by your own code when there is no relationship at play. What sound do you make if you fall in the woods, and nobody is there to hear you? I had no idea how to address that question, so I avoided it as long as I could.

I was actually, to my own detriment, in the complete opposite space. I was hiding my sexuality and, along with it, my individuality. In an effort to get me to come out, my parents pushed me into therapy. They were going to couples counseling at the time and one of the topics of concern was me. Being a big ho, my dad was well versed on where a teenage boy's energy should be directed, and I wasn't bringing any girls around. And the ones that were coming around were clearly just friends. Their couples' counselor recommended a therapist for me. Raylene Goltra was her name. She asked me why my parents had recommended therapy, and when I couldn't come up with an answer, she rattled off a couple go things then suggested, "Maybe you're dealing with your sexuality?" She could see my shocked reaction and immediately started comforting me, telling me about her gay son. She saved my life during those teenage years when suicide seemed like a viable option if nobody in my family was going to accept me in the end. But still, I was not about to come clean at that point. The Persian culture, at least the one of my parents' day, did not by and large approve of homosexuality. It was still something you whispered about in the corner. A source of shame and embarrassment for the entire family. The kind of thing I imagined would crush my father to find out. So even though I was furious with him for cheating and ruining everything, when said therapist, whom my parents had recommended me to, pushed me about being gay, I denied it. My parents may have been ready for me to come out, but I was not. I couldn't hurt my father in that way. I had too much of my mother in me.

Not even MJ knew I was gay. But as graduation faded into the rearview, she knew something was seriously wrong. I'd been eating my feelings and gaining a lot of weight as a result. For a long time, I was relying on food as a suit of armor against the pressures mounting around me. I had learned that making myself overweight had advantages. It shielded me from certain conversations that carry expectations during your high-school years. Being the fat kid, I didn't get questioned about dating and sexuality. When you're that kid, I think people don't look at you or think of you in that way. I think also, and this is gross but probably true, people assume if you're overweight, you don't have the opportunity to date because you're unattractive, so they don't ask you who you have a crush on. They wouldn't want to come across as rude or inappropriate. Overeating was a way, especially as a teenager, to fly under the gay-dar. I didn't even go to prom my senior year because I didn't want to deal with it, and as the chubby kid, like I said, nobody questioned it.

Also, while I'm coming to terms with my sexual urges in my most formative years, there's this whole AIDS thing going on out of nowhere. So, keeping it a secret aside, if I do act on these taboo new urges, I am probably doomed to live a very short and painful life. What's there left to do? I figured I might as well double down on the double-double at In-N-Out because that's the only in and out I'd be getting.

By the time high school was over, I'd come to believe I was a part of too many ostracized groups to have a place anywhere, least of all in America. I graduated in 1991. Know what happened in 1991? Google it. We freakin' invaded Kuwait. It was the start of the first Gulf War! Two decades removed from the hostage crisis and a decade before 9/11, but to most Americans, I still looked like a terrorist. I wasn't comfortable in my own home anymore, or what was left of it, anyway. No safe space there. I really didn't even feel comfortable in the Persian community that had grown around me and become something of a refuge from the accusatory stares of the locals. At that point, all my friends were Persian. I stayed inside this Persian bubble, because that's where the safety and trust were. But now throw "I prefer boys" into the mix, and suddenly, I wouldn't be safe there, either.

It was an awful place to be, both emotionally and physically. I was all bottled up and was starting to have a really fatalistic outlook. The ideas of a successful life, a successful career, a successful relationship—they were all foreign to me. I couldn't imagine what they would even look like. Marriage? *How?* Friends? *Who?* Career? *Why?* In the nightclub of life where everyone's a cocktail, there was no way the Reza on the rocks with a twist didn't get thrown in my own face in the end. I couldn't see happiness beyond my next meal… So, I continued to focus on the meals to get me through my days and it showed more and more. In the age of Schwarzenegger, I had turned myself into Danny DeVito. (No offense Danny. I loved you in *Twins*.)

Thank you, MJ. Thank you for seeing that I needed a spark. To get out of my head and out of my rut. Thank you for knowing your friend needed help. Thank you for making me go to Lifespring.

What is Lifespring, you ask? For those who don't know, Lifespring was a human potential organization back in the seventies, eighties, and nineties. I know what you're thinking, and no, it's not a cult. In a nutshell, it offered a curriculum designed to get people to "stretch" outside of their comfort zones by participating in exercises with each other where they tried different strategies for contending with life situations and saw what new results could be achieved. They steer you away from locking yourself into an outcome based on what you *think* is the way you should deal with something. Okay, so it was kind of like a cult, but whatever. It was what I needed in the moment.

I started to realize that all of the beliefs I'd developed that were forcing me into an emotional cocoon were centered on a single core issue: a lack of trust. Sound familiar? Hello! First with the Shah, then with my dad. I didn't let my guard down around anyone, ever. Food I could trust. Everyone else? No chance. My family, my friends, strangers—God forbid they find out who I really was. I needed a vault for my truth. I would never come out to them. There was no telling how they'd react. No way of seeing it coming. I didn't trust them, and I didn't trust myself to deal with whatever came my way. And through all this distrust, what resulted was a crippling fear.

Here's the thing about fear. Fear is always, at its core, a fear of loss. If you're afraid of letting your significant other out of your sight, it's because you're afraid of losing them. You can be afraid of someone breaking into your house because of what you might lose: your sense of security, your valued possessions, or worse. Afraid to jump out of a plane? You're afraid the chute won't open, and you'll lose your own life. That's why you're also afraid of someone you love jumping out of a plane. You're afraid to lose them. Fear is a loss-based emotion.

My fear of coming out was because I knew I risked losing my standing in the Persian community, my relationships with my parents, and the respect of my friends. You best believe I was keeping my mouth shut with all that on the table. To an eighteen-year-old Persian in Beverly Hills, besides your Cartier LOVE bracelets, what else is there to lose? That's pretty much everything.

In Lifespring, I remember one specific exercise we did. There were about three hundred people—mostly strangers, newbies in the program—standing in a room. We pushed all the chairs back and stacked them against the walls of the banquet hall where the seminar was being held. Our instruction was to walk up to people, look them in the eye, and tell them whether you trust them, don't trust them, or prefer not to say. Choose A, B, or C. In this crowd, there was a guy who looked like a damn killer. Like a straight up homicidal, seventies TV movie–inspired maniac. I'd noticed him earlier in the lobby drinking coffee and having a donut. I remember making a mental note of how he was looking at the other people in the room—like a sushi chef picking over the morning catch, his eyes homing in on each person as he destroyed his donut. You could tell he had a white van in the parking lot and a duffle bag containing nothing but duct tape and a crowbar. It wasn't only the looks he was throwing that got me, either. Uncle Creepy was around fifty at a get-your-life-on-track retreat. Meanwhile I'm eighteen. I'm looking at this guy like he's ancient. Like, "Your tracks are already so close to the cliff, it's too late to hit the brakes, homie."

So, what's he *really* doing here? I'm thinking someone in this room is going to be on the news next week. I'm going to have to give the police sketch artist a visual description for the wanted posters. And now, here we are about to execute a trust exercise. Who would trust this guy? Low and behold, we begin the experiment and shortly after we start mingling, this permed psychopath walks up to me—ME—in a crowd of three hundred people. He's staring at me. I'm pissing myself like, *Oh my gawd I'm the target.* So, to avoid the white van, I tell him I trust him even though I didn't. I figured my reverse psychology might save my life. He then looks me dead in the eye and tells me with his coffee and glazed breath that *he* doesn't trust *me*... Excuse me? *Kiss my ass, Ted Bundy. You have bodies under the floorboard in your house, but you don't trust* me*?*

It may sound like a silly anecdote, but this moment was profound for me. In retrospect, given everything else going on in my life at that point, for this moment to turn the lightbulb on seems semiludicrous. I get a dark vibe from some rando at a cult meeting and it flips a switch? But I swear to you, there's a reason I'm typing this right now. Uncle Creepy changed my outlook on life. This clown knew nothing about me, but he didn't trust me. And all I knew about him was that he was likely eating people like donuts, and I lied and told him I trusted him. It made me think about trust in a whole new way. About the power of trust and how my lack of it shaped my perceptions of the world around me and the decisions I was making about my own attitudes and behaviors. My vigilance. My never wanting to get caught off guard had become crippling to my soul. Based on the lack of trust I had in the people around me, I was living a lie. Trust me, trust is truth. If you don't trust the people closest to you with your truth, you have no authenticity.

It turned out to be a profound exercise for me. It led me to realize my fear of the unknown, or unknowable, was lying to me. Or it was at the very least misrepresenting the stakes. If you're out there struggling with this, if you're keeping something true about yourself hidden from everyone around you, I want you to take this to heart: *your fear of telling the truth is lying to you.* If you are going to lose someone by letting them know who you are, they don't belong in your life to begin with. They are taking up the space that someone who does belong in your life could otherwise occupy. You are not losing anything. Trust, real trust, is everything. You're either going to find out you've gained trust in someone you should have always had it in to begin with or gained the time and space you need for someone you *can* trust to enter your life. You're at risk of losing nothing, so act without fear. If your friends and family can't accept who you truly are, *they* run the risk of losing *you.*

I found out I could trust MJ and a whole lot of other people a lot more than I'd thought. What a feeling of love to suddenly have well up inside you when you realize the people you were afraid would leave had your back the whole time. They were all ride or dies for Reza. I had all this buildup, all this emotional tension I'd been living with for years, hiding and feeling afraid to be my truest self. All of a sudden, it was like Gay Reza was safe, welcomed, and about to be shot out of a cannon at the

Lifespring graduation event. It was going to be this huge dick-shaped cannon and BOOM a plume of rainbow confetti and strobe lights. I'd fly through the air shouting, "I like boys!"

Okay, so there was no cannon. But there was Nick.

Nick, I'd never seen before. He was at the graduation with his friend Valerie, who'd taken part in the class. I laid my freshly outed eyes on Nick, and it was over. Like a vampire watching the sunset for the last time (thank you, Anne Rice), I would never look at boys the same way again. It was a love-at-first-sight type of a deal. Thank god Nick was gay. I might have dusted off the confetti and crawled right back into the cannon, because I was sprung off this dude instantaneously. Remember when I said, when I go to Starbucks, I give the name "Nick" because they can't pronounce "Reza?" Well, that's this Nick. I'm not with him anymore. I'm not even sure where or what he is these days. But I still use his name on the daily. It's a first-love deal for me, I guess.

Nick and I met at the Lifespring graduation, after which we all went out together for drinks. The night went well. Nick and I started hanging out regularly, and before I knew it, we were dating and completely in love. It was a great first relationship for me. It taught me a lot about how being in a functional gay relationship really wasn't any different from being in a functional heterosexual one. Obvious differences aside, of course. The idea that there's a future out there for me with a good relationship and a successful life started to take shape. So, what did I do? I ran away. At least I ran away from Beverly Hills. It was like joining the circus. The big gay circus in nineties' San Francisco. Because here's the thing: Yes, I was being my authentic self. No, I hadn't changed centuries of bias within the Persian community about homosexuality. Beverly Hills was still a Persian bubble to me. I could have stayed in that bubble and gone to college locally, but why? Like I said, changing how I dealt with my sexuality was challenging enough. I didn't need to take on changing the way everyone else dealt with it. Not yet, anyway. Too much, too soon. So, I decided to move to San Francisco—again, a Lifespring-style stretch from my norm—to go to college and see if I couldn't find more people who were accepting of me. Don't worry, I didn't abandon Nick. Not at this point, anyway. When I went off to college, I packed Nick into my suitcase and brought him with me.

San Francisco was an entirely new world. It had new people and new surroundings. It was also the first time in my life I stepped outside my parents' house to live on my own. It was the first time I was free from the energy of an overbearing parent whose unfulfilled dreams I was supposed to manifest. It was the first time I had a sense of, *Oh my God, I don't have to tell anyone where*

I'm going or when I'm coming back. I can come and go as I please. I didn't have to check behind me to see if there was smoke billowing out of the sunroof of an S class. I felt like a grown-up. I wasn't without support, though. I realize now how independent I wasn't. I was still benefiting from my dad being financially responsible for me in a big way.

I had an American Express platinum card that I lived off of at the time. To this day, I keep that card in a giant Cartier jewelry box, along with a lot of other mementos of that time. I'm very sentimental. I collect. I keep. I hold things dear. What's funny though is *that* AmEx platinum card said, "Member since 1980"—I was born in '73. My dad got me my first AmEx before I could ride that primo Diamondback to school on my own. He made sure I was building good credit from the time I was seven years old. So, he had my back in that way for a very long time.

Remember, too, at this time, Dad was getting ready to go live in New York. He could have wiped his hands of me. I was still his only son, though. He was like, "Go find a place in San Francisco. I'll come and sign the lease and do everything." First of all, I was extremely grateful that he was offering to do that. So, I was trying to be responsible. I didn't know San Francisco from a hole in the wall. I didn't know Fisherman's Wharf from The Castro. I flew up there by myself and looked at a bunch of apartments. I found one I was kind of into, that I thought was reasonably priced, and that I could live in. For those of you who know SF, it was near the O'Farrell Theater on Polk Street, which nowadays is fun. But when I was there, it was like Glass-Pipe Central of the crack nineties and I was oblivious. I was a cute, naive Persian kid from a Beverly Hills bubble who got his license to drink and barely drank. Serious fish-out-of-water vibes in New Jack City.

I made an appointment to show my dad this place. My dad flew in, took one look at the apartment, and was like, "Fuck, no." Apologies to the offended, but he was a man of few and four-letter words. That's actually what he said. We got back in his car, drove to Pacific Heights, and he said, "Pick a building." Not to buy. He didn't have it like that. To live in. He literally said, "You won't get murdered in any of these, so pick one." I did. We talked to the manager. Looked at a vacancy. That was it. Dad changed the whole trajectory of the way I thought living in San Francisco was gonna be.

Before that, I was already excited about the move. Now I couldn't wait. My dreams were changing. They were getting really good, actually. Before that, I had this recurring anxiety dream in high school. This was after I started to realize I was gay. In the dream, I would wake up and, somehow, I had been deported back to Iran, imprisoned for being gay, and was dying of full-blown AIDS. It was like three nightmares in one. But dying of AIDS in Iranian prison wasn't the worst of it. In this dream, while all that's going on, I find out that when we were originally fleeing Iran, when I was a baby, they had fucked up on translating my birth certificate. They got my birthday wrong, and it turns out I'm actually a Virgo. A VIRGO! Not a Leo.

Listen, being a Leo was a BIG deal to me. It was the one group where I belonged. I met the only requirement necessary by virtue of my birthday. To be Jewish, your mom has to be Jewish, right? It's matriarchal. To be Muslim, your dad has to be Muslim. It's patriarchal. Well, my mom is Muslim, and my dad is Jewish, so I don't fit in with the Jews or the Muslims. I'm a human oddity with no tribe. Yes, I'm gay, but I wasn't a ho, and I was trying to hide my sexuality. I wasn't cruising the circuit parties wearing Daisy Dukes, shouting, "Hey, girl!" (For the record, I've never been *that* gay.) So, like, even before I came out, I never felt like I fit in with the gays. So, in this nightmare, being a member of this one group (the Leos of the world) that no matter what accepted me as a fellow Leo with no expectations, was gone. Then I would wake up. Not when I was about to die in my dream like a normal person, but when I found out I was a Virgo. That horror was gone thankfully. Now I was dreaming about my inner lion being let loose on the Polk Street Fair.

I had the cool apartment. The BMW convertible. I had direction and motivation. I was on a high like I'd never known.

I'll never forget driving to school from my apartment in Pacific Heights. It took me over Twin Peaks. So, I'm like flying over these hills with the top down in my convertible singing Jodeci at the top of my lungs acapella with the worst voice, enraptured by my surroundings but oblivious to them at the same time. I remember I looked over one day and there was this car next to me, pacing me. They were going the same speed, and they were crying from laughing so hard at me while I frightened seagulls away with my performance of "Come & Talk to Me." They're in tears. And I didn't give a damn. No shame in that game. That's how amazing that felt. For the first time in my life, other people weren't rattling me.

You know the old expression, "It's all good"? It was all good in my hood, seriously. Everything. Driving to school. School. Going to the store was great. Getting gas was great. I had this real sense that, even though I was still living in a major city, it didn't feel congested. The walls weren't closing in. I'd moved to the great outdoors of one of the world's most densely populated cities, but I could spin around in circles with my eyes closed and my arms out and not worry about bumping into anyone or falling off a cliff. Nothing was out of my reach. I've got an American Express card that literally my dad would say, "I got the American Express bill this month."

I'd be like, "Yeah?"

"You spent a lot."

"I did." And that was it. No tirade. No, "You're cut off." No interruption in service of any kind. I had that in LA, but I was strung up like a tether ball. No matter how far I swung in any direction I always landed back in the same place with the same dull clang—the misery of my parents' failed marriage and my internal struggles with my sexuality. That wasn't the case here. Nick was the only thread left of that tether. The last limitation I had. He hadn't always been a limitation, but he became one once everything else was boundless.

CHAPTER 7

NICK AND DICK

Where was Nick while I was learning all the words to *The Sound of Music* for the upcoming sing-along at The Castro Theater? He was right there by my side. At least for a hot minute. Nick was a white Jewish kid from Hidden Hills, the son of an art director and a realtor. He couldn't be more Valley if he tried. He had a relaxed energy that drew me in. A quiet sense of comfort in his skin that was magnetic to me. He was a year younger than I was, a little shorter, trim and handsome, topped with a dollop of curly black hair. He was every bit my first love.

But as chill as he was, there was a chaotic energy that swirled around him. When we first met at that Lifespring graduation, he'd recently been caught by his parents stealing their credit card. Keep in mind we were still in our teens at the time. His parents had sent him to a boarding school in Idyllwild as punishment. Idyllwild is near Palm Springs and a good two-plus-hour drive from Beverly Hills, so distance was something of a barrier in the beginning. On top of that, he'd also recently been in a car accident where one of the other passengers was killed. It wasn't his fault. He wasn't driving. But it was a devastating event. It messed with his emotions and had a physical impact as well. Nick was forced to use a back brace for a very long time.

Looking back, I think there was a piece of me that wanted to save him. We were *so* young when we met. I can barely remember what it was like to be with him to tell the truth. I kind of remember how the whole experience made me feel. I felt in love, but I think it was the idea of him I fell in love with. I wasn't as adept then at judging character or even knowing what qualities I wanted in a partner. I remember he wasn't very affectionate, and that's a big deal to me. I'm a very physical, very tactile person in relationships. I've learned I need to get that back or it makes me feel anxious and unwanted. There were other odds that popped up over time as well. Little things big enough to make him not my person. Still, I was dead set on being with him. Determined as young love is to cross all barriers and defy all odds. Even the ones that shouldn't be stood up to. So, I moved him to San Francisco with me shortly after I went myself. He felt like home in a good way. A security blanket. Something familiar to lean on facing the unknown. Honestly, he could have been everything I'd ever needed in a partner, but it wouldn't have mattered. My life was going to change so much at that point, he could've been the only gay descendant of the Shah himself, and I don't know it would have been enough for me to not get distracted.

Remember, at this point, I've never really lived the gay lifestyle. I was suddenly in the epicenter of the roaring gayties in San Francisco. I'm going to clubs and seeing yummy white hoes prancing around. Then I'd be at the coffee shop the next morning nursing a hangover, and there's more of them there. And different hoes from the ones I saw the night before. They were everywhere. Chiseled, styled, and wild. I hadn't just moved to a more accepting community. This was Babylon. The site of the gold rush and I'd hit the motherload. An infinite supply of hoes everywhere you looked. Hanging off the cable cars. Popping out of the alleys. Seriously, you could find them hiding under your napkin at brunch. It's like someone was printing them. It was an infestation of temptation.

Ah! The tragedy of being a kid in a candy store who's too afraid to taste the lollipops. This was the height of the AIDS crisis. Pop the wrong truffle in your mouth and you might bite right into a razor blade. So, I didn't partake. Pedro Zamora was all over the TV. This handsome Cuban kid was living in the same city I was and telling everyone who would listen that he was dying because he'd had sex with the wrong person. What? Like one false move and that's a wrap? Hell, no. I wasn't about using protection, I was about protecting myself at all costs. I wanted more than anything to be promiscuous and have lots of sex. But how the hell do you roll those dice with a stranger when the stakes are so high? I like orgasms as much as the next guy, but who wants to have sex and die? That's what it was back then. People were having sex and dying from it.

As far as I was concerned, anyone could have HIV and not know it. It was the ultimate watch-your-back. What you don't know will be your downfall scenario.

Also understand that like heteros can be hetero in different ways, there's a whole spectrum of gay out there, too. I knew next to nothing of it at the outset. While it's true your boy is a horn-dog, I'm a certified paranoid germaphobe as well. So, imagine me in the homosexual mecca at the height of the AIDS pandemic in the nineties. Talk about watching your back... I became a top. That's right. For inquiring minds, the rear door to Club Reza is exit only and always has been. I don't want anything in my body that isn't properly seasoned, cooked, and presented. That's my way of being gay.

On top of that, pun intended, I'm a hypochondriac, too. A freakazoid, paranoid germaphobe, hypo. I get a red bump on my hand, I don't brush it off as an ingrown, I jump straight to tick bite and Lyme disease. I'm not kidding. I get grossed out very easily. No mushy strawberries in the crate for me. I'll find another batch. This attitude applies to selecting partners, too. I need to see a manicured appearance. If I see someone who isn't taking care of themselves on the surface—whether it's a missing tooth, grit under the fingernails, or jacked-up shoes—I'll have to pass. Like neatness on a resume, grooming counts! This was all magnified in the early nineties when I was young. I was checking fools off the list with a glance. Especially if they were older and they'd been active in the scene for a long time. To my brain, these veterans likely *did* already have AIDS. So, I wanted to stay clear. I wouldn't even make out with those dudes. If they had a handlebar mustache or a handkerchief or bandanna hanging out of the back pocket of their leather pants, I immediately walked the other way. Flaunting a Village People vibe was like waving a red flag. Understand, there were no treatments or therapeutics at this time. There were guys in advanced stages of the disease roaming the streets of San Francisco. It was a constant visual reminder of the dangers of promiscuity. If you caught it, you had no hope. It destroyed your immune system, and it showed. There were open sores and dramatic weight loss. Physically, you fell apart from the inside out. It made it very easy to not be overly frisky.

Still, I used to have this twisted misconception that if I had less or was less privileged, it would be lit, because I could let loose and not worry about the consequences. I thought my advantages in life and my drive to achieve something great were getting in the way of me wilding out. The irony is, I'd think that about myself, that my life was just too blessed to sacrifice for a good time, then go to the Street Fair and see people cut loose in a way I was envious of and be judgy about it. I'd take on the opposite mentality. Deep down, I was envious of their liberation, but I'd cover it up with thoughts like, *Wow, there's clearly no inheritance in these people's futures. These people are able to live this way because there's nothing to lose. They must be hooked the F up. They aren't even trying to get a government job or show up for work in a suit and tie.* Turns out, this had nothing to do with being gay. I'm a prude when it comes to social appearances. I still sometimes look at other people and wonder what the hell they do for a living that they're able to be the way they are. You've got a giant nose ring, a facial tattoo, and you're walking the streets with a choker around your neck while your partner leads you on a leash. Like, what? You're not afraid to be seen? What if your boss is gay, but isn't *that* kind of gay and he passes by you coming out of a club dressed like that? How does he take you seriously Monday morning when you ask for a raise? This is what goes on in my head.

I came up with this concept that these people must all own

their own businesses. When I see someone on the street, if I call them a small business owner, it's a slang I made up that means I can't imagine them in an office setting. They must have come up with a way to make money for themselves. TikTok, OnlyFans, something is feeding their bank account with no norms attached. Of course, I know the reality is they might all be doctors and lawyers as well. Your personal proclivities have no bearing on your professional abilities. It just still blows my mind. That's all I'm saying.

Even though a wildly promiscuous sex life was off the table for me, I wanted to at least play the game. It looked like too much fun to not participate, even if I never passed Go and collected my two hundred dollars. The problem is, I was still intentionally chubby Reza who was shy about his midsection and felt like he couldn't compete. I said to myself, "Okay, something needs to change." I don't need to worry about the dating-life questions anymore. Everyone knows the deal. The fat armor needs to come off. If I was going to change my surroundings to better my life, I was also going to change my lifestyle and with it my physical appearance. I wanted to look better and feel better about myself in every way. To max out the stock, if you will, and see exactly how high the value goes.

So, I started running and doing that ninety-day come-back kit that was popular at the time. I hit it hard and fast.

The mid-section started to lean. The clothes started to fit and feel different. I'd been wearing strappy tank tops loose to cover myself. Two months in, I'm wearing those same tops tucked into skintight jeans belted with giant belt buckles. The washboard was riding underneath. I was feeling the shit out of myself. And although I wasn't experimenting with sexual partners at this time and didn't want to do anything that would put my long-term plans at risk, I was becoming something of a make-out king and did dabble in drugs a bit. Nothing that involved needles or anything like that. I only wanted to have as much fun as possible.

I discovered ecstasy for the first time living in San Francisco. Two of my friends from LA who were older came to visit and introduced it to me one night when we were bouncing around from club to club. I'll never forget that night or the day after, thanks to that ninety-day comeback kit. As part of that program, they made you journal your food intake. I was using a sheet of paper to keep track of what I was eating. Every day, before I went to bed, I'd sit down and list out all the things I ate that day—this is a practice I actually highly recommend if you're struggling with your weight or your diet and want to gain some control over it. The accountability of making yourself sit there and list out the things you've put in your body forces you to reckon with it. It gives you an opportunity to say, in the moment, when you're in the grocery store holding the Snickers, "Do I want to have to sit there tonight and write this down in my journal?" You don't even have to show the journal to anyone else, knowing you have to face that yourself and own the fact that you let yourself down. There's nothing worse than that feeling. Once you've had to come to grips with the fact that you've let yourself down by doing something as mundane as cheating with Cheetos, it creates a trigger for you. You attach that feeling to the moment of decision when you're thinking of eating something you know you shouldn't. It makes it a lot easier to say no. At least that's what I've found. Anyway, the day I did ecstasy for the first time, the paper had the date and a giant X on it because I ate nothing. Zilch. Not a calorie to be found. For one, ecstasy left me with no appetite, but more than that I was told if you eat while you're on it, it'll diminish the vibe of the drug. That first experience was so amazing to me and so memorable, I didn't want anything tamping it down. That's not to say if you want or need to lose weight that you should take up ecstasy. The journaling will probably suffice. And, yes, I still have that journal. Sentimental AF, remember? I save everything.

So, San Francisco was a first for being out. A first for being on my own. A first for doing drugs. And, as strange as this is going to sound, among all the other firsts, this period was also the very first time I interacted with people who didn't have money. I'd never witnessed firsthand what it meant to be poor.

I mean, I was in class with other people in college who didn't have enough to eat growing up, that kind of poor. When I was a teenager, I was worried that my convertible BMWs weren't new enough or that I should have one more Rolex. I was inundated with privilege. It was all I knew.

This really hit home the first time I had a class where we needed to organize a group study. There were six to seven kids per group, and they were all trying to figure out where they were going to meet outside the class because none of the people had places big enough where six people could fit. My classmates shared their dorms or tiny apartments with roommates. So, I volunteered my place for our group. I lived at 2000 Broadway on the corner of Broadway in Laguna with a view of the Bay. My classmates came over and they were freaking out. It was like someone fed them after midnight and I'd let the Gremlins loose in my crib. They're eating my food, playing Nintendo, smoking on the balcony. They were seriously changing the channels to see what different kinds of shows looked like on a premium quality TV. I was overwhelmed. I didn't know how to feel. Should I be proud or embarrassed? So, I fell back on propriety and started playing host at that point. Making all my mom moves. Making sure nothing breaks and everyone's fed and watered, like she would have done. Then one of these kids comes up to me and pulls me to the side and says, "Listen, we're all trying to figure it out. What is going on here?" I didn't know what he was talking about at first. It threw me, but he went on, "We've come up with two ideas. Your dad is either royalty or an arms dealer." Again, hello, wealthy Persian. Eighteen years old and living like the prince of Fog City. It couldn't be a successful business, or I hit the lottery, or I got an inheritance. It had to be something that matched what they'd seen on TV about Persians. Deposed royalty or terrorist, which one you got? I went with arms dealer. So much sexier than rugs. Kidding, of course.

It was the wake-up call of the century for me. People struggle. People can't go to their doctor when they feel like it, or sometimes even when they really need to. People can't buy whatever they want at the grocery store. I didn't know that was anyone's reality. After that, I would park my car far away from campus. I didn't want anyone to see what I was driving. Not to keep from being robbed or anything like that. I didn't want to make anyone feel bad, and I didn't want anyone to look at me or treat me differently because I was flush. At that stage of life, we were all in the starting block. Nobody had even fired the starting gun yet, and it didn't feel fair.

It also taught me to appreciate what I had and how hard my dad had hustled to provide it for me. That relationship with him, which was so core to my being, which had been so eroded by everything that went on, ticked back a bit because of that. It wasn't that I didn't appreciate what my dad was providing for me before that, but I felt a little, I guess, like he owed it to me because of everything. I don't think I gave him the credit or the respect he deserved for what it took for him to set us up the way he had, if that makes sense. Looking at those other kids and seeing how they were all starting from scratch, I saw some of my dad in them. And was reminded how we, my family, really owed it to him that we had such a great platform to launch from. He might have betrayed the family, but he also built a foundation for us financially, a minimum quality of life, that most other people didn't have or would never experience. It healed a little bit of the wound there. I didn't let him know at the time, because I was still pissed, but it was the beginning of a maturation for me. For the adult I was going to turn into eventually.

Nick was not destined to be a part of that journey. And love him as I once did, I do not have him in a box in my closet. When my self-confidence went up from all the exercise, dieting, and standing on my own two feet, so did my confidence in releasing Nick back into the wild. At that point and at that age, Nick wasn't enough, you know? But I still needed a catalyst to actually pull the trigger. I felt bad. I felt responsible. Here I'd moved this kid whom I already had a savior complex for to San Francisco. I moved him into this baller apartment in Pacific Heights overlooking the Bay. Now, there I was wanting to bail on him. But how? Why? I needed something behind it. A push, excuse, motivation, reason, crutch, whatever you want to call it, that would not be found in San Francisco, but back in the sunny, warm, desert confines of my youth—I'm talking about LA, people.

CHAPTER 8

BEVERLY HOES

I went home for a holiday, or maybe it was to see my family, I'm not 100 percent sure. For some reason, I was back in Beverly Hills for a hot minute, and the hot minute went nuclear. I met Brent. Brent worked at a high-end boutique designer in Beverly Hills with one of my friends. He turned out to be a huge loser, but I had no idea at the time. Some people don't like to talk trash about their exes. Some exes don't deserve to have trash talked about them. But I'm not that person, and Brent is not that ex. He was a total piece of shit. A tall, white, blond cuntbag extraordinaire. Of course, I fell in love with him. Head-over-heels, at-first-sight style. I'm not even exaggerating. On first impression, I thought for sure Brent was the one. Like, THE ONE. I needed to be with him at all costs.

There's-room-on-the-door-next-to-me-while-the-Titanic-sinks-in-the-background style. If I miss this opportunity, I'm going to regret it the rest of my life. Or at least until I bone him.

This chance meeting and overheating gave me the courage to tell Nick I was done, that I was leaving SF, leaving the apartment, unenrolling from school, and breaking up with him. It was a wrap. I was expecting this catastrophic response from Nick. The whole, "How could you scorch my earth like this?" treatment followed by a really uncomfortable process of moving Nick and his shit home with my shit. All while I felt terribly guilty the entire time. Again, I felt responsible for him, so I wasn't going to leave him hanging. I couldn't do that. I was going to get him home to LA. I was going to get him set up in an apartment. I was going to take it right on the chin in this whole long drawn-out speech I prepared. The whole nine. I was thinking a marathon of discomfort was heading my way. The second I started the conversation with Nick, the total opposite happened. I give Nick the letdown. "Hey, so, I think I might be needing to move on and move back to Beverly Hills..." Nick's like, "Cool. I'm staying." And that was it.

Nick got himself an apartment in SF. He moved out. I moved back home. Everything I was worried about never happened. My first love didn't last two years. Godspeed, homie. I wish you all the best. And I'm out.

I moved back to Beverly Hills and immediately started seeing Brent. At first, it was great. I was in the best shape of my life. I'd sunk myself deep into health and fitness, so I went and got a job working as a trainer at a boutique fitness studio, the owner of which was a well-respected, renowned figure in the fitness space. He was a local Hollywood hero. His studio was upscale, and the clientele likewise. It had a family-owned vibe to it because the owner was always around and still worked out of the place himself as a trainer. Before I knew it, I was making decent money, looking peak, and dating a golden god who turned out to be the devil himself.

The relationship with Brent would be the most tumultuous of my life. We didn't get along at all. We were always off and on, then on and off again. We'd take a week break, a two-week break, a month break, but then hook up and get together again. I couldn't quit him, as much as I wanted to, because I had all these confusing emotions at the time keeping me from having any clarity on the situation. Thank goodness the whole fiasco blew up in epic fashion, because it's worth recounting here, which is truly the only value I can still see in it. So here it goes. Why Brent's trash 101:

We were in one of our off-again weeks. I was at work, standing at the reception desk when one of my regulars walked in. They approached me at the desk and said, "Hey Reza, are you and Brent broken up? I saw him at a party last night holding hands with the owner of the studio." The steam coming out of my ears must have fogged the mirror on the wall behind me. "You what?" Did this gossip queen really seriously tell me that my boyfriend, THE ONE, who I'm taking a week-long break from, is out on a date with my damn boss? Hell, no! This is back in the day of landlines—I know, ancient, but the wound is fresh every time I pick at it. I swoop the front-desk phone, the business line, and call Brent. I'm thinking I have to hear this from him first before I dig a deep hole for stacked bodies. *Maybe there's an excuse? Maybe this queen made a mistake?* I'm hoping, sincerely hoping, he did. Either way, I have to know the whole story. So, I call Brent, who answers with a "What's up?" Like he's some dopey beer-brained bro—a red flag if I've ever seen one. Very coolly, and pretty much knowing the answer at that point, I said, "Hey, did you ask my boss out or did *he* ask you out?" No, it wasn't meant to be a trick question. Yes, I assumed guilt. I'm not the justice system. I don't have to presume your innocence if I know you're shady AF to begin with. It's the electric chair until I hear otherwise. Brent, to his slimy credit, didn't dance around it or stammer or try to deny. He straight up said, "He asked me out."

"Okay," I said, "I'll deal with you in a second." I hung up on Brent and called the gym owner, my boss, from the reception phone at his own studio. He answers the phone and confidently I tell him, "I can't work here anymore."

"What are you talking about?"

"Excuse me if you don't know what I'm talking about, but were you out on a date with my sloppy seconds last night?"

This bitch goes, "Do you have a problem with Brent and I being friends?"

"I don't have a problem with you and Brent being friends. I have a problem with you trying to get with my man while we're on a two-week break." (Okay, maybe it was two weeks, not one, but that's beside the point.) I told that dude, straight up, "You're gross, you're old, and I can't fuck with you." *CLICK!* I hung up on him. Then barely took a breath before I called Brent back from that same number and ripped him an asshole he didn't want no matter how good it felt. I did it right in front of one of the other instructors, too. This guy Bob Harper.

Shortly thereafter I started dating Bob.

Bob was a friend prior to this meltdown. We were both trainers at the studio. I was already there when he was hired. When he came into the fold, he brought with him this entire gaggle of fools who thought he was the bees knees. It was like a cult. The cult of Bob. These bitches were obsessed with him. They were fighting over where they were gonna be in the class, calling when the class was full and arguing with reception trying to get into the full class. It was insanity. Meanwhile I was like, *Oh my god! Who is this charismatic mofo who has a following like Moses and shit?* He was an aerobics instructor. And I, wanting to make fast friends with my inspiring new colleague, straight up asked him, "How do you have such a big ass when you're an aerobics instructor?" We both started cracking up.

There was no romantic intent though. I was with Brent at that point, and I don't shit where I eat. Messing around at work, or messing around at your boyfriend's work (ahem, BRENT), is not even in the ballpark of cool with me. So, Bob was hot, but I wasn't going there. Until I *was* going there. After the blow-up, when I quit—and, yes, I sure as hell did—all bets were off. I'm thinking, if I don't have a boyfriend anymore, and I'm not at work anymore at the studio, then let's get to know Bob. I put a target on his big ass. Turns out, I'd need a speed, strength, and conditioning coach to chase down the aerobics instructor. I started taking his classes. I was situating myself close to the front, trying to get some conversation going with him. You know, as one does.

The more I got to know him, the more I started to like him. We ended up becoming best friends. We were inseparable. We'd have lunch together, and we'd work out together every single day. But I'd been firmly planted in the friend zone, which was total bullshit. But I was. All the while I'm thinking, *How do I take this to the next level?* I really wanted more. I was trying so hard. I was monopolizing as much of his time as possible. For whatever reason, it wasn't working. We were getting along great, and it was flirty, but your boy wasn't getting any action outside the classroom.

Then, one day, we're standing around talking after class and one of the other guys in the class says, out of the blue, "You guys should get it over with and have sex already. You act like you've had sex. Have sex." Thank GAWD! So, I literally said to Bob, "Look, everyone thinks we've had sex. Why can't we just have sex?"

He didn't say no.

I booked a hotel room at L'Ermitage on Burton Way in Beverly Hills. It's a schmancy, Hollywood hideaway. There are always movie stars and other entertainment industry types frequenting the bar off the lobby. It's called the Writer's Bar. They have framed screenplays from classic motion pictures hanging on the wall. Dim lighting. It's a very warm, elevated vibe. It carries over to the rooms, too. Low-to-the-ground, platform king beds. Jacuzzi tub in the bathroom. The rooms feel more like a spa retreat than a hotel room in a bustling metropolis. Hollywood Zen in Beverly Hills. It wasn't cheap, but I was finally getting my man. I wasn't about to pinch pennies when I had plenty of other things to squeeze between my fingers. I got a bottle of Cristal, a bottle of Dom. I got white grapes, red grapes, and some of the other usual suspects for this kind of rendezvous.

Earmuffs, Adam. What a night.

I got there early. I filled up the bathtub. I took a bath. I set the mood. I lit what must have been a hundred of those little votive candles. I seriously made it into a shrine for the cult of Bob. I was about to get something everyone else in the cult dreamed they could have. The Diamondback bicycle of booty, my aerobics instructor. He finally arrived and everything was amazing. It surpassed my wildest fantasies. It's still one of the most memorable experiences of my life. Without getting into too much detail, which seems off-tone, or should we say the wrong content for this book's rating, at some point in the evening we got really hungry. I grabbed the phone and called down to order room service. I'm talking to this person in the kitchen, I'm putting in the order, but before I can finish the line goes dead. Out of nowhere, I can no longer hear the person on the other end. Odd… I'm about to hang up and try again when I realize the food will have to wait. There's something more urgent to attend to. I'd been dangling the phone cord over one of my little votive candles and had set it on fire. I freaked out. I launched, screaming, from the bed, inadvertently sweeping more candles off the nightstand, dumping wax everywhere. One of them lands on my pillow and burns a hole in it. I'm scrambling around the room trying to put out these little fires. I accidentally kicked the platform bed, which is of course flush to the ground. I kicked it full force, too, and I broke two of my toes. No joke. I was wailing in pain. The room was a mini inferno. Bob was cracking up. This whole dream date turned into the most expensive hookup ever. Between the medical for my toes, the damage to the room, the food, the champagne, and the cost of the room itself, there's no question—Bob cost me more than anyone else, but I'll be damned if we didn't make it count. It was worth it! And it was not the finish line. It was the start of something great.

Bob and I carried on like that for a good while. It was very much a friends-with-benefits situation, though. I wanted more, but I always got the feeling he wasn't interested in any kind of serious relationship with anybody, so I didn't really push the matter.

One day I called the studio to schedule his aerobics class. It was day-of, last minute, but usually that wasn't a problem for me. I had some VIP status going on. They told me, "Bob's not teaching today." I said, "Why not? I've got the schedule. He's listed."

"Bob's getting married." *He what?* That sapsucker got married. Not to me, either. To some guy named Scott who I'd never met and didn't know existed! Guard down. Backstabbed again!

If you think a little thing like that was going to deter me, you haven't been paying attention. I had my heart and my mind set on that fool. So, what did I do? I became best friends with him *and* his husband. And our affair went on like it was no big deal that he'd tied the knot. We still did everything together, but now we were a threesome. We even traveled together. We went to Hawaii together, the three of us, and I hit it aloha style in the next room. I'm not kidding. Bob and I still ended up falling totally in love. For a while, Bob was bouncing back and forth between Scott and me. As far as I was concerned, I was still in the game.

The end of this story is a bit bittersweet. Poor Scott, who I honestly harbored no ill will toward even though I was chasing his husband, ended up passing away. And even though Bob and I didn't last forever, we remain friends to this day. I actually sold Bob's house for him a few months ago.

At the time though, Bob was the catalyst for me to realize that this is not okay. For me, I mean. Second place is not enough. It should never have been enough for me to want so badly to be with someone or to have someone or to love someone whom I had to fight so hard for. They weren't giving me what I needed or wanted. They weren't even really giving me the respect I deserved. I really wanted to have a stable, long-term relationship with someone who was loving and loyal to me and only me. Someone who was choosing to be with me above all others, and not out of desperation, either. Someone who had options, but was still choosing me. Someone who was nothing like my father as far as relationships went.

I had a friend named Zeke, who at the time was also a personal trainer. Training was his side hustle, though. He was also a professional dancer. Not like on weekends or on tables, but a professional, legitimate entertainment dancer. He got hired right after I broke it off with Bob to go on tour with Ricky Martin. So, he was globe-trotting all over the place, and I was back in Beverly Hills licking my wounds and trying to figure out where I kept going wrong. Meanwhile, I'm in touch with Zeke, and he keeps telling me to come visit. Come to Spain. Come to Paris. Come here. Come there. I would say no to everywhere. I wasn't having it. It felt like more trouble than it was worth. I didn't know anybody but him anywhere he was. I don't speak French. I don't speak Spanish. "You'll be working the whole time." No. No. No.

Finally, when it was London, he said, "Come to London." And I was like, "Okay they speak English. I can roll with that." *When Zeke is rehearsing, I can run around, do my thing, and get along great.* So, I go, and as it turns out, to make the whole thing even better, one of my personal training clients, Jefferey, was in London at the same time. *Great! I get to hang out with Jefferey while I'm there, too.*

One day, Zeke was training. Jeffrey and I decided to go have lunch at a spot called Balans on Old Compton Street in what is essentially the WeHo (West Hollywood) of London. Their version of Boystown. We're sitting there downing bangers and mash, and this guy walks by and Jefferey says, "Oh my God, I know that guy. I met him at a party last time I was here." He pops out of his chair to go say hi to this random hot Brazilian named Dennis who then continues on his way. My first thought was, *Brazilian named Dennis? How did that happen? The name Dennis was even retired by white people decades ago. How did it end up in Brazil?*

Jefferey doesn't say another word about Dennis. He sits back down. We keep eating and move on. Then when we finish lunch, Jefferey says, "Dennis is at a coffee shop down the street. Do you want to go have a coffee?" *Do I want to go have coffee with a hot Brazilian named Dennis who lives in London and is learning English?* Suddenly my fear of not being able to communicate melts away, and I of course say, "Yes, please. Let's go meet Dennis."

Halfway through my latte, I'm in love with Dennis. We hang out the whole time I'm in London. It was a total whirlwind rebound romance. It's still going strong when it's time for me to go back to the States. I'm thinking, *Well, that was fun.* I really liked this dude, but the long-distance thing didn't necessarily feel like it was going to work. Then it did. We kept dating while he was in London, and I was home in the States. He ended up coming to visit me. Things were going great. I'm thinking, *Okay, this is it. We need to get married.* Well, not we but he. He needs to get married so he can stay in the States and keep dating me. So, I bought him a wife. Yes, I'm that guy. I paid something like ten Gs to this friend of mine, who I was really close to, to marry Dennis so he could get a green card. It all worked out. Everything was going as well as it could until I started having an affair with my younger cousin's best friend.

Okay, before you crucify your boy, or think shittier of me, let me break it down. This was later. I had moved Dennis in and had been living with him for some time. The relationship had kinda run its course, and I was feeling pretty miserable about it. But in true Reza twenties and thirties fashion, I feel responsible for him because he moved from London to live in LA to be with me, the whole deal. (Hello, sound familiar, anybody? I know, repeated patterns. I wasn't seeing it yet, though.) Anyway, I didn't know how to tell Dennis that I was happy he'd upended his life for me, but that I wanted to bounce. So, I did the next worse thing. I cheated.

I'd moved on from personal training at this point. I was still in shape, but now I had a realtor license and was starting to make some real-real money. I was living life in suits instead of sweats, pimping a whole different professional vibe. One day, I'm on the ground floor of Luckman Plaza, a high-rise on Sunset

Boulevard, where my office was located. I was at the café in the lobby ordering lunch when this guy comes up to me and starts touching me on the shoulder. First of all, *ew!* Who randomly puts their hands on strangers in line at a café? You know how I am about germs at this point, and how baseline contagious I believe every other human on the planet is. Then here's this strange, possibly contaminated hand on my shoulder.

"Is your name Reza?"

What? He knows me? Today, I wouldn't bat an eye. I've got some celebrity going for me. I'm no Harry Syles, but I do get recognized and talked to randomly on the street from time to time. Back then, though, I was a handsome burgeoning Persian realtor. Which in Beverly Hills is like saying, "I live in Beverly Hills." It's entirely populated with Persian realtors and the people whose homes they've sold.

Hoping I can end the physical contact with tone, I said in the most off-putting and suspicious way possible, "Yeah?" He proceeds to introduce himself as my cousin Ali's best friend. His name is Sean. And, potential contagions aside, the guy was gorgeous and much younger than me. By like a decade at first glance. Let me tell you something in case you don't know. Getting hit on by someone that young and beautiful makes you feel young and beautiful all over again. It was a new feeling to me and one I couldn't resist. I ran with it. We had lunch together that day. We talked. We got along. We became friends. We started hanging out all the time. We start having an affair. Eventually he shares that he's in love with me.

It was horrendous.

Horrendous because I thought I was in love with him, too, but I still had Brazilian Dennis as a live-in and still felt more guilty about potentially sending him packing than I did about cheating on him. *What to do?* I set my boy toy up in another place, of course, where I can meet with him whenever I want. Being a real estate agent, I'd also become a real estate investor. I owned a place in Tamarisk West in Rancho Mirage. That's Palm Springs adjacent for the uninitiated. It's about two hours east of Beverly Hills and a gay mecca to this day. If WeHo is Boystown, Palm Springs is boy's oasis. So, I got Sean all set up as my side-piece at my weekend getaway in the desert. Sean knew about Dennis, so he was cool with leaving no trace so we wouldn't get found out whenever Dennis was in the desert.

It was hot and heavy for a hot minute, then the whole house of cards burned to the ground. I was there in the desert with Sean. It was during the week. I had made some excuse to Dennis about needing to meet someone for business, so he didn't question me being out of town. Meanwhile, Sean and I were hooking up. Dennis was planning to join me in the desert on Friday so we could spend the weekend together. Sean and I shuffled everything around in the apartment, so none of Sean's incriminating presence would be detected. Sean got out before Dennis came in. It was no problem. Dennis arrived, I played it all off, he was none the wiser. Everything was going smoothly until some bad timing and some dumb shit by me blew it all up in my face. I left my phone sitting out while I was in the shower. Sean sent me a text. "I wish you were still inside of me," or some dirty shit like that. Dennis saw the message from Sean pop up on my phone. Game over. Dennis didn't take it lightly. This was not like the Nick situation. Dennis was still in love and had no idea I was not. He and I went at it full throttle. The tears were flowing. The emotions were firing. I don't know what I was thinking at the time, but Dennis talked me out of Sean and talked me back into him. That's right. By the end of this bloodletting, I was back on team Dennis. Dennis and I decided we were gonna try and work things out.

We started going to couples' counseling together. I was saying all the right things. I was trying to feel it even though I still wasn't feeling it. For the record, I was still seeing Sean on the side. I couldn't quit him, either. As this is being drug out, Dennis and I ended up going to Brazil together to spend time with his family. This was maybe the second or third time we took a trip like that. I knew his family well. While we were there, we tried to have sex. Dennis lost his erection. I asked him what was wrong. He said point-blank, "I don't think I'm in love with you anymore." *Are you F-ing kidding me, dude?!* Here I was forcing myself to be in this relationship because I felt like I was responsible for him... Where have you heard that before? I made him move to the United States and get married to some random girl so he would have citizenship and be able to live with me. Now, here he was, unable to get hard because he didn't love me. *Geezus. Fine. Perfect. We're done.* We went home and that was it. I was totally cool with it. There wasn't a hint of remorse or regret. There were no unresolved feelings. Everything was fine...until I started dividing the sock drawer. Our socks were in the same drawer in the master closet. Separating the socks, I lost it. I started bawling. All this emotion that had been bundled up and suppressed for whatever reason boiled over. Here I thought I was getting out of this cold. I wasn't. It hurt in a way I wasn't anticipating. I didn't want to be with Dennis anymore, but I really had loved him for a time, and I think in that moment I realized what I'd lost. Not the person, but the feeling I had for that person. That feeling of being in love. Knee to The Righteous Brothers by way of Tom Cruise in *Top Gun*, I'd lost that loving feeling.

Anyway, I got Dennis an apartment. I paid the first year of rent for him. That was it. Flash forward more than a decade, Adam and I were recently at his holiday party in Studio City. We met Dennis's new partner, who looks like a Latin version of me, and, get this, he's a *Leo*. Just saying... Adam, meanwhile, looks like a Dennis, but nothing like a Brazilian one.

You're probably wondering, at least I hope you are, what happened to Sean. In a word, Mom. Wednesday nights when Dennis and I were together, we had a standing date where we would go to my mom's for dinner. Mind you, I haven't told her anything about any of this entanglement. No mama, no drama, fo sho. Until one particular, or should I say *notorious*, Wednesday I go over to my mom's for dinner on date night and Dennis isn't with me. Mom wants to know where Dennis is. She loved Dennis. I laid the whole situation out to her. I tell her about Sean. The incident in Rancho Mirage, the incident in Brazil. I told her the whole story. This is days before Dennis physically moved out of my house for the last time. Mom goes, "Get in the car." I'm like, "What? I'm here for dinner."

"Get in the car," she said.

We get in the car. We go back to my house. Dennis is there. Mom sends me to my room—in my own house! I'm a grown-ass man, and she sent me to my room. She wanted to have a talk with Dennis. Fine. Honestly, I didn't even want to be a part of it. I had a TV. There were snacks in the fridge. To hell with dinner. "Have at it, Mom." I vanish upstairs.

I'm minding my own business. They're down there for what feels like hours. God knows what happened. I don't want to know. Eventually she summons me downstairs and tells me to walk her to her car. Nothing else. I'm not even sure where Dennis disappeared to at the time, but he's no longer with her and in some other part of the house. As I'm walking her out, she pretty much ends my relationship with Sean. She knew all about who Sean was. Remember he was besties with my cousin. So, she knew him. She knew he was a sly little hookery troublemaker. She says to me, "You're making the biggest mistake of your life, and that little bitch [Sean] has no room in our family. Whatever you gotta do, do it. But don't think he's ever gonna get accepted around here." She got in her car and straight peeled out. The smoke. The smell of burned rubber. "Dang, Mom!" She wasn't messing around.

She wasn't wrong, either. I kinda knew. Here I was, a successful adult with a good business and income. I had some investment properties. So...yeah. I straight up said to Sean, "I can't date you anymore. My mom doesn't like you." Of course he didn't understand why. Me, though, I knew. What was I going to say if someone asked me where my boyfriend lived? "Oh, he lives at home with his parents when I'm not banging him in Rancho Mirage." I couldn't anymore. I needed to live in my reality and stop clinging to this fantasy idea of the beautiful young boy who made me feel young again.

If you can't read between the lines with these romances, let me explain it for you. I have an innate ability to make things in my head seem better than they are in real life. It's the double-edged sword of always being able to see the silver lining. I could live comfortably on the silver lining and never acknowledge that I was in the clouds. Remember that cloud that followed Schleprock everywhere? The one I thought followed me? Yeah, I ended up living on that cloud, and I'd learned to give that bitch a silver lining. It was Reza's silver lining, and it went wherever I did. It's become a fixed part of my being over the years. Sometimes it amplifies something that's kinda good to begin with. Like, if I'm at dinner and I'm eating something really good, I'll be so enthusiastic about it, it will make the other people at the table actually hate what they're eating. I know it's weird, but I swear it's how I am now. I have fallen completely in love with simply being. For the most part, it's a harmless proclivity toward enjoying every day that has led me at times to try to prop up a broken status quo instead of letting it move on its own time so that something greater could come along.

Let me tell you something I learned in therapy: We all seek out familiarity in adulthood. We find it comforting, even if it's harmful. My home life growing up had been tumultuous because my parents came from different sides of the track. The Jew and the Muslim. They were star-crossed lovers. There was an irreconcilable conflict at the root of their relationship. Then once my dad started cheating, and they stayed together, the tension between sides became more stressed and wounding. Recounting my pre-Adam past now, it's pretty clear that I was in some way at home with difficult relationships. There was always some hurdle that needed to be overcome. I not only embraced but sought out that tension because it was familiar to me, so I felt confident in that space. I knew how to navigate it because it's the road I traveled in my most formative years. I fought through it. I suffered at times because of it: He was too young, and he was my cousin's best friend. He lived in London and needed a green card. He was married to someone else. He was an asshole whom I couldn't stand but couldn't get away from until he hooked up with my boss. He was injured in a car accident, had no money, and was living hours away from me. It was never easy. Then one day it was. And I didn't trust it because I was so unfamiliar with it. Until I forced myself to venture out into the uncharted territory of a comfortable relationship. I realize now, comfort, security, safety, those were the things I craved, even though what I'd been attracted to was the exact opposite. So how do you find your way off the only path you've ever walked? You need a guide. I needed someone who could convince me that when it comes to relationships, the tunnel of love can be more exciting than the roller coaster. Praise the lord for Adam.

Wait, wait, wait… Before we get to Adam, you need to hear about Trey. The only reason Adam exists is because of Trey…

I met Trey at the office. I know I have a don't-shit-where-you-eat rule, but sticking to it hadn't served me all that well. Nothing had. So, F it. He was trying to be a realtor. He was trying to be an actor, too. He looked more like an actor and acted more like a realtor. Go figure. I was crazy about him. He was prototypically everything I was not. The anti-me, if you will.

He was performing in a play at the time. (I don't like plays and have no interest in pretending to be someone I'm not.) He went to Burning Man. (I haven't worked as hard as I have to be successful so that I can spend a week miserable in the middle of a blazing desert while pretending I have no money.) He played guitar and drove a red Subaru station wagon. (Subaru is *not* Mercedes.) He only wore flannel. (Flannel may be flammable, but that doesn't make it hot.) He had a Shiba Inu named Scout that went everywhere with him. (I'm a cat person.)

Maybe it was still the old star-crossed lovers thing. They say opposites attract. But this time the only barriers were superficial. There was no crisis at the core of the relationship, but rather different vibes.

Those granola vibes turned out to be the exact energy I needed in my life. A calming laidback influence. The embodiment of my soulmate in the wrong body. My goodness, though;

it was like a lightbulb went off. Trey wasn't the right fit for me in a lot of ways. Our personalities and interests weren't as aligned as they needed to be. However, I figured out with Trey what I needed from a relationship in my life. An actor taught me that I needed to avoid drama. So, what did I do? I found a way subconsciously to conjure up drama where there was none. I got carried away. I was enamored with Trey. So much so that I had a wedding invitation, something I'd made myself on the computer, a DIY wedding invitation, printed out and pinned to my bulletin board at my office. That's my energy. Trey saw it.

He freaked out. So, while Trey was the type of energy I needed in my life, I was not the type of energy Trey needed. I totally Bridezilla'd that poor guy before we even got to the engagement. I was so in love with him and obsessed with how he made me feel. I thought I'd found my muse. The missing piece of me. He was this monotone, homebody, attention-be-damned dude cruising the river of life on the dry side of a leaf. I didn't possess any of that. I'm always the cause in the cause-and-effect equation of the universe. Having someone I couldn't rattle made me realize how great that type of unflappable, reliable, salt-of-the-earth steadiness was to me. He was the rock to my kite. He could keep me from floating off into the stratosphere. He was a herald of the gods bringing me the message I needed to hear to prepare me for what was to come. But after he saw the wedding invitation, he was past tense.

We realized we weren't on the same page. He didn't want what I wanted, not now, nor anytime soon, so we broke up.

Now I knew, though. Not what I didn't want. That's so often the easy part. You have to go farther. I had that miracle experience that put my inner child on the same page with the outward adult. I was armed with the elixir for what ailed me. I knew what I wanted. Mind you, I had no idea where else to look for it. I don't mean geographically. You can Google Map Venice, California, drive down there, and chuck a rock into the air, and it'll land on a pretty gay boy who has worn a flannel shirt, and nothing else, to Burning Man where they played guitar and ate granola, and nothing else, for a week straight. I mean, I needed all that in a person who I connected with. A true love who was simultaneously grounding, unflappable, and interested in a long-term relationship with yours truly.

At the time, though, the end of the relationship with Trey really messed up my head. Trey and I broke up shortly before my thirty-fifth birthday. In the wake of that breakup, Trey went back to his ex-boyfriend. That had never happened to me before. It made me feel like everything I'd experienced with Trey was a lie in some way. I really was hollow in that moment and feeling like there was no point in even trying anymore. I'd seriously spent twenty years—*twenty*—from the time I was fifteen and started having romantic feelings to thirty-five. I had this World War I trench warfare aftermath from relationships in my rearview mirror. Now I found someone who had everything I knew I needed, and he dumped me to get back with his ex. *Seriously, dude?*

Life came full circle for me at my thirty-fifth birthday party. I had this big, lavish party at this duplex I owned with a coworker named Pamela. It had a pool and a spa in the yard. I was so psyched. Then the day of the party, we realized Pamela left the pool heater on too long and the pool was too hot to get into. It was boiling hot. You could brew tea in the pool. It was ridiculous. So, my party planner had to order these huge blocks of ice to drop into the pool to cool it down. I kid you not, it cost thousands of dollars to chill the pool we'd spent hundreds of dollars heating. Needless to say, I kind of went into the night on a little bit of a damper, but of course I wasn't going to show it, right? And honestly the party was a blast.

Everyone was there. Dennis came. Sean came. (We actually hooked up that night for the last time—I needed a rebound!) Trey and his ex-now-again-lover showed up, dropped off a bottle of wine, and left—not to be assholes, because by the time they got there, which was very late, the party had turned into an orgy, and everyone was naked in the jacuzzi. People (besides me) were having full-on sex in front of everyone. It was crazy. There was a DJ on the balcony facing the backyard. The bar we rented was acrylic and hollow. So, the party planner put pictures of me inside. There was a taco truck. It was a party you throw one time and never again. It was amazing.

Then I woke up the next day and realized that was it. That party was as good as life was going to get. I told myself, *Reza, you're never going to find your person. Every high will be followed shortly after by a low. You've somehow wandered onto a roller coaster of your own design that you never intended to build, but now you are stuck on it.* I could see the tunnel of love. All my exes were riding that shit. And here I was going one more round on the coaster. Great. At least I had my silver lining. I still had fun the night before. But that life I so desperately had searched for was never going to be found. This was new territory for me. I'd never been the person I was the morning after my thirty-fifth birthday before. Sometime later, I learned that the human body transforms itself completely every seven years. Your body is always in the process of expunging existing cells and replenishing them with new ones. This cycle of rejuvenation takes about seven years. Think about that. Every seven years you're a completely different physical body than the one that began the previous seven-year cycle. Here I was at thirty-five, experiencing this sensation, at the end of the previous seven-year cycle and about to begin the next one. I was resigned to my fate, and about to be caught off guard in the best possible way.

CHAPTER 9

UP IN ADAM

I'm living at that duplex, selling real estate, and going to Gold's Gym. I am what I am. I've got what I've got. It's not what I wanted, but not the worst thing that could happen to you. I have the same distance from birth as I do from seventy and from what I can see, I'm running in place. Literally. I'm on a treadmill at Gold's Gym, running in place, and I'm wearing big, noise-canceling, DJ-style headphones so that nobody will bother me. The idea that I will one day be a celebrity of sorts and the subject of a television show weren't even in my field of vision. Neither was this goofy-looking white boy who crept up on me mid-stride and says, "Hey."

"Hey."

"You know my friend Britt."

"No, I don't."

He starts arguing. "Yes, you do."

"I don't. I don't know anyone named Britt."

"You totally do."

I'm like, "Bitch, I don't know anyone named Britt."

I literally called this milkweed dude a bitch and in response, he starts telling me his life's story. Seriously. He skips right over "bitch" and "Britt" and goes into how he's doing some internship over here and doing some other thing over there, and I'm thinking, *White people are crazy. Like what the hell is going on right now?* They walk up to you and start telling you about all the shit they're doing as a come-on? Is that how it's done where you come from? I wouldn't tell some rando on a treadmill what I'm up to in life or where I'm interning. What if they're psychotic? What if they follow me to my internship? I watch an obsessive amount of true crime documentaries. Do white people not? (Side note, true crime seriously ought to be taught in high school, if you ask me. Home economics first period, home invasion second period. There's a big blind spot for some people when it comes to how frequently sociopaths pop up in society. I digress.) So, this *Dennis the Menace* type finally gives up the ghost and leaves me alone having gotten absolutely nowhere. I didn't think anything more of it, aside from double-checking under the car before I left the gym to make sure he wasn't trying to pull some *Cape Fear* shit on me. I go about my life. But the next time I'm at Gold's Gym, there he is. I see this dorky white guy again. Sure enough, he's making a beeline for me with a dorky look on his face. He comes up to me and shows me a picture on his phone from some gay pride event where there're a bunch of people at a bar. I'm in this group shot—like a random group photo at gay pride. He points out that his friend Britt is also in the photo. I don't know this ho. I'm thinking, *Do you know how many people are in photos at gay pride that I'm also in? Do you know how social media works? We don't exchange phone numbers and hang out afterward.* I don't say any of that of course, because as dorky as he is, I'm thinking *he's not going to understand any of it*. I'm also thinking, *he's taller and younger than Trey, and he's clearly hitting on me, so I might as well own whatever he wants me to own and hook up with him.* Milkweed's name was Adam… As if you could get any more fundamental than that.

Adam, when I met him, had two pairs of shoes. One was a pair of gray Converse All Stars that he would wear every day, until they got so worn down and trashy looking that he was forced to go to the store and purchase a *new* pair of gray Converse All Stars. He would then wear those until they got too ratty and force him to repeat the cycle. Adam had worn gray Converse All Stars every day of his adult life. His second pair of shoes were still athletic shoes, mind you, but leather ones. So slightly nicer. He had those in case he ever had to go somewhere that gray Converse All Stars were too casual for. But since Adam never went anywhere he deemed too fancy for gray Converse All Stars, he never wore the other pair of shoes. Adam, in a word, was uncomplicated. He didn't have a mother that was one religion, a father that was another religion, a country he fled from. No husband. No kids. No injuries. He was a U.S. citizen. He lived in my zip code. He wasn't afraid of commitment. He had none of that, and he had one pair of shoes.

Monotony was not, and is not, boring to Adam. Monotony is the spice of Adam's life. Why add salt and pepper to your salad when just salt will do? *Dum–Tee–Dum–Tee–Dum–Tee–Dum–Tee*... That's the soundtrack to Adam's life. It precedes him everywhere he goes. You can hear it in the air before he walks into view. He has one expression to go with his shoes: a goofy smile. It's always on his face. He's always amiable and pleased to see you. He's a human Labrador. In flannel. I seriously wouldn't have it any other way. I'm crazy, uppity, anxious, and overwrought sometimes. But then I take one look at Adam, I hear his music, and it calms me down. Adam moves through life with a contagious oblivion to detail. He's a walking quaalude. When we were first dating, I was vegan for about eighteen months—a fact that he was fully aware of. Yet when it was his turn to do dinner, he'd bring home pork tenderloin from Trader

Joe's. I'll never forget it. F-ing pork tenderloin. I know you've seen one. This fleshly, footlong, tube of raw pig, vacuum sealed in plastic. I'd be like, "What's for dinner, honey?" *Whale dick, you vegan pussy, you want it roasted or barbecued?*

First of all, as we've established, I'm half-Muslim and half-Jewish, so pork hasn't been a big part of my life growing up. I don't even eat dark meat chicken, let alone pork tenderloin. And at this point in my life, I didn't even eat dairy. None of that would register with him when he'd be standing in the store looking at the meat section and deciding that's what he wanted to cook for dinner, though. He wasn't being malicious. It's like he didn't understand or had his own governing list of priorities. Like you can be totally vegan, sure, but tonight you're downing a whale dick, no biggie. Eleven, dare I say, twelve years into our marriage, Adam and I are still the same couple we've always been. Except now *he's* vegan, the son of a bitch, and I have to be sensitive to it when I'm planning the menu. We have like fifty vegan cookbooks on the shelf. As I'm writing this, he's planning a dinner of tofu nuggets, breaded and barbecued, with hot sauce on them. Meanwhile I'm over here craving a cheeseburger and not caring. Because I'd rather do something we both want to do. I'd rather be part of this perfectly blended orchestra than break out into an obnoxious solo. We still joke with each other nonstop. We have to pretend to not get along sometimes to mix things up. We both start acting bitchy. I call him Queen. He calls me Queen. That's the music we make together.

Adam's an amazing contradiction in terms. He doesn't pay attention to detail like I do, because most things aren't important enough to him to prioritize that kind of attention. He goes the extra mile and a half in every way a person could, to incorporate and appreciate so many of the details that make up me. He really zeroes in and gives great thought to who I am emotionally and intellectually. He respects and studies my culture. He's generous and warm toward my family. He learned to speak Farsi. He's into our holidays and understands our traditions. He really involves himself in my family's life. It's how he expresses affection. They, in turn, love him. It's really wonderful. I always FaceTime with my mom at night. This one time, Adam casually (but very intentionally) walked by in the background and yelled at my mom, "I'm a Jew!" My mom and I were cracking up, because he had converted to Judaism for me. So, he shouted, "I'm a Jew!" and exited stage left without a second beat. He's hysterical once you get to know him and understand his sense of humor. I'm not sure that ever came across on the show, but you all should know that. Adam is subtle, but he's legit the business.

I have a cousin who's gay and like eight to ten years younger than me. I'm not exactly sure how old, but that's beside the point. He's still living it up and bouncing from one one-night stand to the next. I don't begrudge or envy him. He was asking me how I ended up getting married and staying happily married. He knows I used to be where he is now, before I met Adam. Everyone he dates ends up annoying him in some way because he's so high-strung and particular about everything. He was telling me how he can't see himself living with someone else for any length of time. He needs his own space governed by his own rules, undisturbed. I used to be the exact same way. At the same time, nobody—well, most people—fancies the idea of growing old alone and never settling down. So cellular regeneration every seven years aside, he wanted to know how I got myself to a place where I could fathom living in the same space and breathing the same air as someone else, day in and day out. I gave him this advice, and now I'm passing it along to you. If you're in a similar space and you aren't meeting the one, or you're feeling like you'll never meet someone whom you'll gel with all the time, maybe you're so set in who you are that you don't know how you'll ever be able to compromise and meet someone else part way. I'll say to you now what I said to him then. You're right to feel that way because it's true. You'll never meet anyone who doesn't annoy you from time to time and whom you gel with all the time. Stop thinking that's going to change or that that feeling needs to change for you to cohabitate. Instead, you have to learn what I learned: how to not let little annoyances outweigh or overpower all the positive things you appreciate about that special someone. I had to learn to appreciate Adam in that way, and you will too if you ever expect to get or stay married.

There's a song that I'm sure most of you are familiar with, and the lyrics go, "Move, bitch! Get out the way! Get out the way!" You can google it if you haven't heard of it and listen to it now before you continue reading if you wish, but Chris Rock does this bit where he's making fun of that song. He talks about learning to get the proverbial bitches out of your way in order to achieve, whatever it is… I feel like that's the best way for me to explain how I got to that place in my own life and in my relationship with Adam. Whatever my own issues were (those proverbial bitches) that were blocking me from being able to fully embrace everything it meant to be in a relationship with Adam. That was my work to do on myself, not his job to change. He's been the same wonderful person throughout our relationship. He didn't all of a sudden become better. I've learned over time to calm the F down. Not every reaction you have is important. Your feelings can be valid without being all-powerful. They're only overpowering if you give them that power. If some petty annoyance is going to totally rule over your relationship, that's a personal issue, partner. You need to get real with yourself. Say it out loud: "That's my problem. Not a big deal." Don't overreact or get mad at someone you love for not replacing the toilet paper roll if they use the last bit of it. Waddle over to the vanity, get another roll, and move on.

Being as particular as I am, I had a lot of personal bitches I had to move outta my way. Once that work was done, though, I tapped fully into how great Adam the person and Adam the husband was. Those are the things that are important. It really doesn't matter if he's the best housemate.

I think a lot of those particulars are really defense mechanisms, anyway. They're excuses you give yourself in order to shield people from getting too close to you. I had to let my guard down completely with Adam and embrace everything about him. Once I realized that was on me to do, not on him to coax out of me, I realized, *Oh, shit! This is amazing. Adam is truly amazing.*

Having someone and trusting them and knowing that they're gonna come through for you the way you would come through for them is amazing. Knowing that even if they don't, if they let you down because that's inevitable in any relationship, that doesn't mean you have to get upset at them. Give your husband, wife, significant other, dog, cat, parrot, whoever it is... Give them the grace you would give yourself. Do not do unto others what you would find repulsive if done to yourself. Sometimes we forget how all-encompassing the golden rule is, and we apply it to our smallest or most inconsequential relationships while forgetting to make it the foundational block of our most important ones. Remember, we all struggle at times to live up to not only the expectations of our loved ones but of ourselves. Think about how many times you've let yourself down. Other people are going to do that, too. It doesn't mean you cast them off and condemn them anymore than you would do to yourself.

Here's more advice, if you're struggling with this. The next time your significant other does something you think is messed up and you feel yourself getting really upset with that person, remind yourself, if you did that, you wouldn't want your significant other to get upset with you. So, you should probably not get upset with them. It's that simple. If whatever they've done passes that test, don't get upset. Don't take it out on them. Get over it and move on. It took me years of therapy to get there, so if it takes you a few times, don't panic. It takes practice to put yourself in check and calm yourself down before you react in a way that hurts someone you care about over something that means very little at the end of the day. Adam doesn't need to do things like I do them. Whether it's folding the towels properly, filling up the tank before bringing the car home, or not making roasted whale dick for a vegan dinner. Let it go. Even if Adam's way of doing something is lame as hell, dumb as shit, slower than black tar molasses, makes no damn sense from front to back, and doesn't net as good of a result as my way would have... I need to let him do his thing. Eye roll, yes, but with lids closed to protect his feelings. That annoyance belongs to me, not him. That's my shit, and the love of my life doesn't need me flinging it at him like some petulant chimp in the peanut gallery at the LA zoo.

Marriage is about companionship. You know that old saying, "Laugh and the world laughs with you, but cry and you cry alone"? Whoever said that BS wasn't in a happy marriage. Alone my ass. A good husband or wife is there when the tears start flowing like nobody else. After an eleven-year investment into my marriage with Adam, I cashed all my stocks in when my dad passed away.

It's March 2023 as I'm writing this. I've laid the second-most important man in my life to rest. You want to talk about crying? The floodgates opened when my dad died. Losing a parent is something you can't fully comprehend until you go through it. It makes you reevaluate a lot of things. The best I can do, if you've yet to experience the loss of a parent, is to tell you that all the cliché shit your parents tell you about life when you're growing up... It all rings true the day they die.

When it first happened, when I got that call letting me know he was gone, I was in a state of shock, I think. It didn't come out of the blue. Dad's health had been deteriorating rapidly for months. His mental and physical capacities were being torn apart by dementia. He was living in a memory care facility. We could see the end coming, so when I say shock, I don't mean it was a surprise; I mean that it stunned my entire system. I was stone-cold. I looked like I had leapt straight to the acceptance stage of grief, but in fact, I was very much still in the denial phase and did not know. Something inside of me was holding the pain at bay.

It was befuddling, maybe even in a subconscious way, to see this man who had always been so much bigger than life reduced the way he was toward the end. The man whose appearance meant so much to him was now unbothered by it. A man whose appetite for life was so voracious and whose drive to achieve and acquire had so defined him in my mind. Now here he was limited in scope by the four walls of this facility.

Seeing him like that, a tremendous amount of regret welled up inside of me. I had given him hell for betraying my mom and our family for the sake of sidepieces. I hated him at times for it. Dismissed him. He seemed impregnable to my disgust, and that only made him all the more a target. His invulnerability justified my ire in a way. But he was no longer formidable. No longer even the conscious author of his own actions. I visited him often in that facility, and seeing him like that, I started to wonder to what degree he had ever been in charge of himself.

The guilt, the missed opportunity, would ultimately be gutting. Those emotions didn't fully hit me until we were making the video montage for the funeral service. We were going through old photos of my dad. There was his life. All of it. Laid out from beginning to end. Seeing him in that light made it a lot easier for me to be compassionate toward him for everything he had to deal with and how he reacted. We know our parents' lives impact our own. I think most people, to some degree, feel like their childhoods should have been better. Or could have been better had their parents done things differently. I know I'm guilty of this. But how often do we consider who they are as people apart from us? It's easy to see Adam as a friend, a spouse, a housemate to me, and then to stand back and also see him as an uncle, a son-in-law, or even an employee. I see how he plays all these different roles. It's different with parents, though. I always looked at my dad through the lens of him being my dad. As if that's all he ever was, even though he'd lived almost half his life before I was ever born. All those people he'd been before he was my dad were still a part of who he was when he *was also* my dad. Looking through those photos of his childhood and his wedding in Iran, I started to see his life not only from the point of view of the role I played in it. I saw the entirety of my father. I saw him as a child with a challenging and abandoning mother. I saw a man who ventured out of the boundaries of his own religion at a time when people didn't really do that. I saw him as a man younger than I was when he found true love in a woman, my mother. She was standing next to me in tears. She was still here. Where she had come from, and who she was as a Muslim, were as far from my dad's childhood as he could get. He was running away from his own upbringing when he married her.

I saw him as a young professional. A man gaining incredible knowledge about rugs and business. Someone acutely attentive to detail with a remarkable talent for memory. He's who I got that from. Who he was is genetically ingrained in me. He was someone who built generational wealth and then was forced to flee his life and rebuild it. He did that. How many people would have rolled over, gone belly-up, and crawled into a bottle? He kept fighting. He had to become a refugee from his homeland as a midlife crisis. I grew up in Beverly Hills. I'm still here! That wasn't his home, but he made it mine. God bless him. He could have succumbed to family pressures and religious pressures. He didn't. He fought and fought and fought again. I started to see him as someone who had overcome so much in his life to provide me with so much. Who am I to judge him for some of the things he did later in life that maybe weren't in our best interest? For whatever reason, he felt he had to do those things for himself. Maybe he did feel guilty about it. Maybe he stayed with my mom long after he wanted to because he felt responsible for her. Maybe all those flings he had were really only flings, but deep down he felt a sense of responsibility to those side hoes, too. He felt he owed them in the same way he owed my mom. My gawd, maybe my dad felt exactly how I did and did exactly the same things I did. I felt responsible for Nick, for Dennis, for Sean... Had I sought out people I needed to take care of, or did I feel like it was the right thing to do? Maybe my dad felt the exact same way. The only difference is that I wasn't married with kids. And my dad did these things to my mom, and that's the only reason I had any platform on which to stand in judgment over him. If my dad had been gay, maybe he'd have lived the exact same life I did and treated his various liaisons exactly how I did.

Did I really condemn him for being who I was and doing all these things that I've also done? Was I really going to sit here and say he never should have gotten married and had kids if he didn't want to own that commitment? Maybe he tried and failed. Maybe he got married too young. Maybe all the pressure he was dealing with caused him to step out on my mom. The truth is, I don't know. He took all that to the grave with him because I never thought to ask those questions until it was too late. I got mad and judged him instead.

I was able to forgive him after he died in a way that felt like maybe I should have forgiven him sooner. No, not maybe. That's not fair to him or to myself. I wish I'd forgiven him sooner. That's a very hard thing for me to say and to come to terms with. I feel a lot of regret for the way I treated my dad. I don't like feeling regretful. Regret is my least favorite emotion. I really hate it. I regret not asking my dad more questions. I regret never trying to understand his side of his story. I regret that I can't write about what he was feeling, thinking, or needing when he left my mom because I don't know any of that. I never asked.

Hindsight gives you clarity on a lot of things. When he moved to New York, he would ask me a question, I would answer it, then later in the conversation he would ask me the same question again. I always thought he wasn't paying attention to me. Like he was too busy living his life and doing his own thing. I'd think to myself, *He's calling me out of obligation. It's not something he actually wants to do. He doesn't even pay attention to me.* It turns out his Alzheimer's was probably already a part of his world, and I didn't recognize it or care enough to think past *my* own nose. I could have asked him why he was forgetting everything. I could have simply been straightforward myself and said to him, "Dad, you just asked me that question." Instead, I let it irritate me. I bottled it up. It made me angry at him when I shouldn't have been. I get that I didn't have all the information, but I didn't have it not because he hadn't bothered, but because I hadn't. I wasn't showing him any compassion. I was treating him the way I treated everybody, with my guard up. In assuming he was being inconsiderate of me, I wasn't being considerate of him, and that was the wrong thing to do.

Your parents are a part of 100 percent of your life until they're gone. But for your parents, when you're a kid, you're a small percentage of the life they've already lived. My dad was in his thirties when I was born, so for like the first eight years or so of my life, I really was occupying like 25 percent of my dad's experiences. If that. If you think about it that way, my dad has always known way more about who I was than I knew about who he was. I feel like I should have given more consideration to everything he was besides my dad.

At the end of the day, though, I know the bond we had, that had been frayed, could never be destroyed. Maybe that's the story for dads and sons. Maybe we never figure it all out until it's too late, and that's the way it goes. There was this one moment, when he was in memory care, I'm definitely going to hold onto, though. If it were tangible, I'd put it in one of those boxes in my closet, but since it only exists now in my memory, I'm going to leave it here:

When I was little, my dad used to snap at me with his teeth. It was something playful he'd do with a smile. If I was messing with him, or tugging at him, or being a pain in the butt, he'd whip his head at me like a velociraptor and clack his teeth together as if he was trying to bite me. It was always meant in good fun, of course. I'd giggle. He'd smile. As the end was getting near, my dad had started to grind his teeth a lot. It was awful. It made this terrible sound that was painful to listen to. He'd lay there in bed, unable to communicate, sounding like coral trees in high wind, the wood bending and crackling as if they're being torn apart and are about to topple. I was trying to get him to stop doing it. I knew he couldn't help it, but I thought maybe if I massaged his jaw muscles—you know, that bulge where the jaw hinges in front of and below the ears—maybe I could ease whatever tension that was causing him to do it. So, I'm sitting with him and massaging his jaw and talking to him about the good ol' days. I was trying to be loving and reassuring. Letting him know how much I care about him. He whipped his face at my hand and snapped at it in that same playful way he used to. He hadn't done that for decades, but in that moment, everything else that had gone on, all the water that had washed under the bridge, was dried up. He was my dad again, nothing more. He was 100 percent my dad. He made me giggle. He smiled.

In his room, where they had his name and other information like his chart, he had stickers and stars like you'd get on your kindergarten homework for being a good patient. This was crazy to me. My dad was a lot of things, but being cooperative wasn't one of them. This guy who was so ferocious when I was a kid was now docile and agreeable? He had these care providers convinced he was kind and easygoing? The teacher's pet? He was the guy everyone loved above all the other patients? Him? Talk about a salesman. My dad to the last.

Losing a parent makes you want to be a better human. But not in a vacuum. In all the roles you fill in other peoples' lives. A better brother, a better son, a better friend, a better colleague, a better husband. Whether someone cuts you off, or someone's not as nice at the coffee shop, or you're inconvenienced. Anytime you set an expectation and it's not met, my advice is tone it down, you know? Bring it down a notch before you react. Your expectations belong to you and you alone. They're your bitches, and sometimes they need to get out the way.

Ultimately, I've learned to give myself the same grace I want to give others. I was on a reality TV show for the past decade, so I've been put on edge in a way I had never experienced before. As many good things as reality TV brings into your life, it brings as many, if not more, negative things. It takes up so much space. I was so caught up in that aspect of my life that I was mentally checked out more than I should have been everywhere else. I'm definitely guilty of that, but I also know now, looking back, it couldn't have totally been helped.

That brings me back to Adam, because he and I got together right before the show happened. He's been with me through all of it. So, when my cousin told me you can be happy and live a fulfilling life single, I understood it. Yeah, you can be happy and fulfilled, but life isn't all happiness and fulfillment. There's so much more to it. The thought of coming home from that memorial service that night to an empty house, that would have been awful. I would've felt like shit. I would've stayed in the shit. I would have ruminated on it. Nothing would've shaken me from it. I didn't have to do that, though. I'm married. I've got Adam. He was able to be there for me in such a profound way I cannot express my gratitude enough. He helped me grieve. He was supportive. He helped me come up. I honestly don't know if you can come up from such overpowering grief if there's no one there to help you.

Adam makes even the mundane things fun to the point where most things aren't as interesting or fun as staying home and watching TV, cuddling, talking, cooking, doing little tasks or projects around the house, playing cards or games, playing with our animals, etc. You want to know what a good marriage, once you let the insignificant stuff go, can be like? No matter what else is going on, I only want to hang out with Adam. That's what it's like.

CHAPTER 10

SULTANS OF SUNSET

Tell me you want to cast me on a TV show, and I'll tell you I have better things to do with my time than have smoke blown up my rear by some flimsy Tinseltown stage-fiver. That was my mindset over a decade ago. I'm talking 2010. If you don't or have never lived in and around the entertainment industry, you're going to have to trust me. If you live in La-La Land long enough, more than one person will flatter you with the promise of fame. "You're so cute. You should be in a boy band." "You're so funny. You should do stand-up." "You're so photogenic. Your eyebrows belong on a magazine cover." I've heard them all, and I've taken each and every one with the same grain of stale salt. The one that never manages to make it out of my grinder before I refill it.

So, you know, flattery and grandiose promises are not the way to my heart. On the contrary, they always make my spidey sense tingle. I generally assume unwarranted compliments are part of a larger con and that I should immediately cling tightly to my wallet with both hands. If someone in Hollywood is telling you how awesome you are and how they can do all kinds of great things for you, it probably really means they think they can manipulate you into doing something for them. Don't try selling ice to this Inuit, honey. We live in a desert, and I can afford a fridge. So, when MJ called and said something about our mutual friend Sammy's friend Marissa having a boyfriend who thought it would be a good idea to showcase Iranian culture in a reality show in Beverly Hills, I balked. "Can't you and I go grab a drink?" I'm down for MJ and bourbon on the rocks, why do we have to entertain all the other *Spaceballs* nonsense about your father's brother's sister's cousin's former roommate being an aspiring whatever? MJ thickened the plot with the fact that this boyfriend worked at Ryan Seacrest Productions—*Oh, good. He can drop a name, too? How original.*—and that he hadn't spent a lot of time around Persians before he started dating Marissa, but now he thinks our culture and how we live and our philosophies and everything were unique and interesting and might make a good show. I still simply wanted the drink and some MJ time, so when she added, "Come over and hang out. We'll have some wine and cheese and stuff." Okay, while I'm nobody's fool, I *am* a sucker for three things: wine, cheese, and the company of good friends. So, I got behind the wheel and went on my merry way to capitalize on all three.

I have wine, cheese, and MJ to thank for so much of the best things that have happened in my life, and this was to be the topper. Driving to that meeting, I had no idea it was the first leg of a journey that would take me through the next decade and change my life forever. If I had, I'd probably have been driving three times the speed. This was to be the ride of a lifetime.

On the surface, it sounded implausible for anyone in power in Hollywood to dedicate an hour time slot and a production budget to showcasing a bunch of well-to-do middle-aged Iranians. Contrarily, I also remember thinking *My Big Fat Greek Wedding* was a big hit, and that was basically a showcase for Greek culture. Why not Persians, too? Maybe there is a small appetite out there that they (the proverbial "they" of the Hollywood power structure) could tap into. I wouldn't say I had a spark of hope or anything like that. It was more like I could see the Duraflame and the fireplace and thought, *I guess there's the potential for fire.*

I got to MJ's spot. Sammy was there. Marissa and MJ and this boyfriend/wannabe television producer were there. His name was Jesse. He seemed polite and nice enough if not a dynamo of charisma and potential. He wasn't the kind of guy who could make dreams come true with a flick of his wand at this point in his career. Anyway, we lube up the night with a bottle of Cab and some Gruyère-topped Raincoast crisps, and we got to talking about what it would take to win ourselves a prove-it deal for a Persian reality show. We needed to figure out what the focus of the show might be. Should it be about families or singles? If it's about families, should it be one family or two? Everyone started telling stories from our own lives as a way to spitball the overall approach. Jesse was throwing in his two cents and in a way shaping the conversation and pushing the concepts. We didn't come out of the night with all the answers. Not by a long shot. Jesse, being the one who was going to sell it, had a sense of what buyers would want to see and hear, but he hadn't yet heard it all. I do remember he said to me that night, "If I'm going to make this thing work, I'm going to need you to be the funny gay guy." However the rest of this was going to go down, he saw how I would be defined and what my part in shaping the show would be. Basically, he wanted me to be myself. I *am* a funny gay guy. That's no stretch. I was like, "Yeah, cool. Sounds great." I left the night with strong opinions about the charcuterie but not much in the way of hope that a TV show starring yours truly was going to pan out. So many of these types of conversations happen when you live near the business, but most of them never get so much as a follow-up.

But then there was a follow-up. Several. Sammy was hitting me up and filling me in on what Jesse was doing to move the project forward. He wouldn't let it go. Whatever he was doing, he hadn't lost interest in, including me. It started to feel like he was really committed to his idea that he wanted to put Persian culture front and center in prime time. *Maybe this whole thing did have some legs?*

I still wasn't having any delusions of grandeur, but at the very least, I no longer had my guard up. I wasn't being asked to do anything or contribute anything. I was still part of the plan. It wasn't entirely implausible no matter how unlikely. Which is a good way to describe pretty much anything and everything that's ever come out of the entertainment industry. Not entirely implausible, but unlikely.

If you're considering a run at show business of any kind, the only thing I can tell you that's 100 percent true is this: The only way to move from unlikely to likely is to do something about it. I don't know exactly what Jesse was doing, but he was doing *something*.

One day, Jesse called me directly, a little out of the blue, and told me he wanted to shoot a sizzle reel. For the uninitiated, a sizzle reel is a proof of concept. A down-and-dirty, grassroots, let's skip the permits and the budget, hit Record on some cameras, follow you guys around until some fun stuff happens, then cut it together way of getting a greenlight. It's done to show the people in power what's possible. It had been months since our little get-together. This was the logical next step. The fact that it was still moving, and now moving into some tangible direction, was interesting if not thrilling. I was still thinking about it the way one imagines winning the lottery, but at least I wasn't going to a convenience store smelling of stale coffee and nacho cheese to drop five on it. I was being asked to go shopping on Rodeo Drive with my friends while an entourage taped us. All the while I would try to be the most charming and entertaining version of myself. Again, just living, but now with a guerrilla crew. I wasn't thirsty for it. I sure as hell wasn't banking on it.

If it seems like I was being too dismissive or unappreciative at this point, remember, I was already working in real estate by this time. I'd also recently hit a closing milestone. It was my first house that sold over $5 million. I was like, "Boom! I have arrived. I'm getting myself back for this one."

So, I went out and purchased my absolute, number one, favorite watch in life: the all-gold Rolex Daytona. I wasn't some dewy-eyed teen, Kansas transplant. I was thirty-eight years old, already rolling with the Rollie on my arm. I'd had multiple careers where I had seen success. The most recent had me flush. I also had Adam on lock and a lifetime of growth in the rearview. I was cool. I wasn't awed by Jesse, I was thinking, *This climber probably lives in an 800-square-foot apartment. Like, how's he going to lift me up?* This whole TV show thing, for me, was something that somebody else was pursuing on my behalf. I didn't really have skin in the game. He's telling me I'll need to get a lawyer to negotiate my contract, and I'm thinking, *Does this rube really look at me and think I don't have a lawyer?* Come on, now.

The timing felt odd to me, too. *You're seriously pushing Persians into the limelight right now?* Arab Spring was happening in Egypt and across the Middle East. It was a full-blown uprising of millions of people. The status quo in the Middle East was getting a lot of negative attention due to these protests and the threat of civil war from all these people demanding free elections, economic freedom, human rights, etc. And on top of that, the United States military had brought Osama bin Laden to justice. That was all over the news. There was this cathartic moment for everyone who'd been impacted by the nightmare on 9/11. And once again, people who looked like me were being featured as terrorists and theocrats and scary old men with white wizard beards on every screen in the country. *This is a lot of noise to try to shout over the top of*, I thought.

All that isn't to say I didn't want it to happen. I was actually planning on it happening. I was manifesting the hell out of it. I had all this pent-up emotion and experience that I wanted to let the world know about. I knew being Persian had nothing to do with what was going on in Iran. Iran is a geographically bounded country, now run by lunatic religious zealots. I was from Iran. And I was Persian, yes. But I considered myself Persian American. I grew up here, homie. I wanted to let the damn Ayatollah know I was alive and well. I wanted to let everyday people know everything they'd come to believe about what it meant to be from Iran was wrong. I'm the counterprogramming to the twenty-four-hour news cycle. I'm the rest of the story. Not only that, I'm the best part of it. The uplifting part. If you want to see the whole picture, you need to see me.

So, I knew I wanted and needed a platform. I wasn't yet convinced this was the way it was going to happen. Shopping on Rodeo Drive is cool, but if they wanted a TV show, we needed to do more than walk around with no permits or license or anything, trying to get some B-roll glamour shots of us holding Hermes bags and shit. That wasn't gonna be the ticket. They needed to let me say what I had to say. Which brings me to that fateful day when Jesse sat me down and we did a mock confessional to add to the reel. I knew if I nailed that, it'd be a wrap. Spoiler alert, for years after we were on the air, I heard that my mock confessional moment was something still being talked about across the Bravoverse. It wasn't the whole expedition. I'm not claiming that or trying to take away from everyone's contributions or anything. But that damn well sank the hook.

The day of, I planned out every detail from what I wanted to let people know down to the wardrobe details. That was the day the character of Reza was born. Not that I wasn't going to be myself. It was more an idea that I could amplify myself for the sake of entertaining people. If you take who I really am, and turn the volume up to eleven, you'll get someone the world would be drawn to. I wore these pink and white seersucker shorts, and I wore a pink shirt and a pink bow tie. I had my legs out and I was wearing Gucci leather loafers with no socks. We had a Persian sculpture behind me, a little guy I still have in my house to this day. He was on the dresser behind me. We put a Persian rug out and a hookah samovar.

So, you've got this traditional Persian backdrop, and all the assumptions that come with it. You think you know what kind of person lives in that environment. You have these notions. Then there's me, decked out like some East Coast senator's niece vacationing in the Hamptons. With a bow tie and a mustache. Flamboyant. Articulate. Persian. Half-Jewish. Half-Muslim. Went to high school with Monica Lewinsky and Eric Menendez. Oh, and as gay as St. Patty's Day. How could I not captivate the audience? I have a very unique perspective on everything by definition. I'm a rare species of mofo, seriously endangered in most of the world, and here they are releasing me into the wild and training a camera lens on my ass. If I'm the orator, if I'm the storyteller, I don't have to invent anything to be compelling. All I have to do is share my authentic life. How I think, what I do, all of that. It was in my head. It's a whole world that's never been explored on television. Virgin territory, irony intended. Who wouldn't be curious about my perspective?

That day, I was able to change the way the project would be viewed. I was going to focus on the positive and show everyone in the world, including those assholes who stole our country back in the seventies, that they may have won a battle, but they lost the war. This show wasn't going to be like some National Geographic expedition on the plight of the Persian. We were going to be able to let viewers see, hear, taste, and touch everything that it means to *us* to be Persian. That pre-revolution Persian culture: affluent, opulent, progressive, prosperous, badass. This was happening thirty-four years after the fall of the Shah, and they were still dealing with the same garbage they were dealing with in the seventies. The unrest. The dictatorship. The theocracy. The oppression. They're *still* dealing with it today. If you haven't watched the news lately, people are still being murdered by the government, and rebellions and protests are still upsetting the cart. Literally nothing has changed.

Meanwhile, in the States, lives and livelihoods are rebuilt. Families are growing. Communities are thriving. That lavish lifestyle was about to hit the airwaves. We had everything we needed to create a show that would show the world what it was like to be from the Persia we remembered. The Shah's Persia.

We could broadcast to the world that everything the Ayatollah and his followers fought so hard to destroy and bury was alive and well and up on the biggest screens there were. And in prime time, bitch. You want the anti-Ayatollah? I'm your man to the damn bone. You want someone to shove it up that old bastard's nose? I was the person to do it. The gay (you hate that) American (you hate that) fan of King Mohammed Reza Shah (you hated him) who would be one of the loudest spokespeople in the world for how awesome and alive everything you hate still is and in the fanciest place on the damn planet—the 90210.

As that confessional taping went on, I got more and more confident that I could be an integral part of something powerful through this vehicle. People would dig my mustache and laugh at how funny I was and how wild my friend group was. Every episode would be entertaining and aspirational, and in being that, it would be the biggest possible middle finger to all of Mohammad Reza Shah's enemies. Through me, he could get the last laugh and the final word. So, by all means, let's call it *Sultans of Sunset*. Wait, what? Yes. That's what they wanted to call it. Until we explained to them that there were no sultans in Iran, and that none of us wanted to be sultans. We all wanted to be, and were about to become, shahs.

This occurred, of course, after they took our sizzle and ran it through test audience, after focus group, after executive panel to determine whether or not Americans were ready to watch and follow Persians on a TV show. Talk about a reality check. What do you mean, America might not be ready for us? We ARE America, homie. I couldn't believe these producer types were openly talking about this with us, as if it was a totally cool way to view it and talk about it. Tell me you think the show doesn't work or isn't funny enough or needs to be more about this or that. Don't tell me you think the sizzle is amazing but that you're worried Americans aren't "ready" for Persians to be on TV. I was over it; you should be, too. I know damn well the people whose minds you're trying to read will be into it, and I already told you why, so put it down on tape. Thankfully for everyone concerned, those focus groups didn't disappoint. They confirmed what we knew. The world was ready.

However, I wasn't ready quite yet. In my head and heart, I felt like I'd get a lot of support publicly and win America over. But that's not a given. As much headway as the gay community has made in terms of acceptance, there are still those out there, even in a country as progressive as the United States, who would simply get rid of all of us if they could, Ayatollah style. Thank god, the law is not on their side here the way it is in the Middle East. That doesn't mean outlaws wouldn't still, or don't still, condone, or worse, carry out violence against people in the gay community.

What would I be inviting into my life, Adam's life (we were together at this time, though not yet married), my family's life? There are real stakes if this doesn't go over well. Any animosity harbored by bigots against me for being gay might be doubly so because I'm also Middle Eastern.

As concerned, if not afraid, about this as I was, my mom was maybe triply so. She was concerned about the safety of her son, you know? I'm her spoiled angel. Her baby prince. She's not one to keep her two cents to herself as it is, and in this instance, she was pulling stress out of the ATM in twenties. Her big fear was that not only would the show basically bomb and go nowhere, but that all I would get for my trouble was a lot of hate. Not only nationally, but locally. Remember the Persian community as a whole is still not the most inviting of the gay lifestyle, either. What if some asshole decided I was making a mockery of Persians and wanted to make an example out of me? What if I tanked my booming real estate career by going on this cheap and cheerful reality show and coming off like a clown? All we had were six episodes. It's not like there was some big financial incentive to go this route. There was a lot at stake, and my mother made sure to remind me the entire time about how bad this could go. She wasn't being negative to be hurtful; she was being protective, and I get that. Also, I was in a good place with my dad at this time, too. We'd done a lot of work healing that relationship. I think he'd come to terms with the fact his son was gay, and he was getting over it. What if he got pissed that I broadcast this very personal part of his life nationally and caused him problems? I didn't want to do that, either. There was a lot to weigh.

At the end of the day, though, I had faith in myself, and I had a hope to achieve something greater. For my family, I wanted them to not only be *okay* with the fact I was gay, but I wanted to give them something more than validation. I wanted to actually do something that made them proud of me in a way that transcended my sexuality. I wanted to be an ambassador for them, for the country they lost, and for the culture they fought so hard to preserve. And I'm not going to sugarcoat it and act like it was all altruism and love. F that. I wanted to raise a big fat middle finger to Ahmadinejad, the ignorant president of Iran who actually made the claim publicly that there were no gay Iranians. So, there was the sociological experiment piece of it for me, too. I had a hypothesis I wanted to test. Could I be funny enough, warm enough, and genuine enough to make people who were opposed to homosexuality decide that gay isn't as bad as they thought?

This wasn't the Reza show—though I'd argue it turned into

that at least for that first season. If my little experiment with the lofty goals was going to work, the rest of the cast would have to work. Thinking from my own point of view, if I was going to come across as my best self, I'd need to be surrounded by people that would allow me to be that person.

CHAPTER 11

CAST YOUR PEARLS

Cast is everything in reality TV, and we hadn't yet settled on ours. We had three cast members locked in at that point—me, MJ, and Sammy—and we'd all been friends prior to the show, so chemistry wasn't an issue. Mike was added shortly after. We met him at Jesse's house, and quickly realized that the four of us could work well together, so he became part of the core group at that point. Asa and Golnesa came on the show with a few other folks who ultimately ended up either being removed or given more ancillary roles in season one. The magic of television part of this is that we weren't all friends prior to being brought together for the show. However, once we knew it was a go, we all started hanging out with each other obsessively. It was like the show *Love Is Blind* but instead of dating in a pod, it was friendship in a pod. These people became my entire world. It was like being initiated into a cult with no ramp-up. You're in it, and you better be a fanatical believer ready to do work when called upon. So, by the time the cameras were up, you're like, *I've known these people my whole life. I know everything about them.*

Two years. That's about how long it was from that initial meeting with Jesse to the time season one aired. If that sounds like a long time, it is. The wheels turn slowly in entertainment. By the time the show was ready to be unleashed, it already had a lot of pushback built up in the local Persian community. The animosity was somewhat unexpected, but not totally surprising. The Persian community is very insulated and protective of itself in a good way, but it is also cliquish and exclusive in a bad way. A lot of talking heads who'd caught wind of what we were doing were already mounting their defense. *All the noise they are creating*, I thought, *is great for us*. It was going to make the show even bigger. We knew what we were doing was going to get good attention, so the bad attention was a bonus.

I remember the former mayor of Beverly Hills Jimmy Delshad, who was the first Persian to ever hold public office in Beverly Hills, came out against it. You'd think of all people, he'd be all about promoting Persian culture. Nope. He started talking trash publicly about us. I remember thinking to myself, *Jimmy, you need to stay in your lane, homie*. Your roots might be in

Iran, but your roots aren't showing; you're a dyed-in-the-wool politician. First of all, your name is Jamshid, so I don't know why you need to be Jimmy to anyone. Second, your children don't speak Farsi. They don't eat Persian food. And don't get me started on your wife. I'd never say it out loud, but I think she legally changed her middle name to Sale Rack. So don't come at me when you don't know me.

That was the Beverly Hills crowd. West Hollywood was worse. The two are adjacent, if you don't know, and a lot of the less fortunate, less successful Persians settled in West Hollywood. That's also what we call Boystown, and there's a big gay population and a lot of gay bars and clubs in that area. They were all talking trash, too. They were seriously going to the city council, trying to make decrees against us. Like, "You can't have permits to shoot your show in our area." It was amazing. There was so much press. There were psychologists and sociologists going on Persian AM radio. There was this billboard-having, ambulance-chasing attorney speaking out against us. People were up in arms over our little soon-to-be six-episode season one that they hadn't even seen. You could not have asked for better free publicity. I am eternally grateful to all the haters for coming out of the woodwork. Not only did it help get the word out, but it also motivated everyone on the cast to make sure we did our part to get a season two. A decade later, how ya like us now? Your kids probably line up at Bravocon to get a picture with me, wearing the Reza costume they started selling for Halloween. I'm not even kidding. Look it up. It had a T-shirt that looked like a button up, with the top buttons undone and a hairy chest poking out. It came with my mustache. It was hysterical. Season one dealt a lot with me and my going to New York to visit my dad. At times it felt like the Reza show. At least it did to me. I was loving it. Who doesn't want their own Halloween costume at Spirit Halloween?

We were an immediate hit, but we didn't really know it. Credit the culture at Bravo in those days—or more broadly, I guess, the business of reality TV. The last thing they want is for the cast to figure out how valuable they are. They want to keep you in the dark and keep a thumb on your head, so you don't ask for more money. There's no gold statue moment. It's a constant game of trying to keep you in check no matter how popular you become. Also, we're investing our own money to promote ourselves and our lifestyle. So, I was out buying Louboutins to maintain the image, meanwhile my checks weren't even covering the price of the shoes.

With how dumpy everything about the production was at that point, my minuscule check felt like it might be eating up the majority of the budget. During season one, I shot my confessional interviews in a storage closet. I'm not even kidding. Go back and watch. It's all blurred out. They got some wooden boxes and put Persian-ish tchotchkes on it. There's a cheap red plastic chandelier that looks like a refugee from a Mandarin dollhouse. And let me tell you, there was no air-conditioning there. With the lights—and it was middle of summer—I was purging under my suit. It was so bad, I started buying bags of ice that I would put under my bare feet to cool myself off as I was talking. Funnier, sometimes the janitor would actually walk in and need supplies from the closet that we were shooting in. So, we would have to stop the camera, because even though we had a permit, he had right of way. The camera person was doing my makeup, for God's sake. We didn't have a legit makeup artist. She bought some cosmetics and kept them with her. She would help us put them on before we shot.

Another thing, because they wanted us drinking at all times—nothing like a little social lubricant to pump up the volume—we weren't allowed to drive from place to place. So, they gave us taxi vouchers. We got these vouchers, and we soon realized, if you told the cabbie that you were going to use the voucher, they wouldn't pick you up. It's apparently a lot of paperwork for them if they accept these vouchers, and they don't want to do it. So, you had to call them, get in, wait till you got to your destination, then pop the voucher on them. I really felt bad about it, because we knew they hated it, but there was nothing else we could do at that point.

The way we were shooting this show, the standards by which we were shooting it, were way below the standards we were living by. That's something I think people don't understand about making a TV show. When you're starting it, it's really like starting a small business and hoping it will at some point grow into something profitable. But in the beginning, you're cutting every corner you can to save a nickel, because there's a chance the whole thing could blow up in your face and end up costing the production company a lot of money if it's not a success.

The other thing about it, too, as it goes on and does start making money, you start feeling like you've now got a successful business you've helped build, but they want to make sure you know you're not in control. It's not your business. It's theirs. You're a contractor. Even if your ratings are good, they make you sweat over getting picked up for another season. It doesn't matter if it's season two or season ten, you don't know until it feels like everyone else in the world does that you're coming back for another season. They basically tell you right before you start shooting to limit the amount of time you have to negotiate your salary.

On paper, mind you, they lock you in. They make you sign so that you're committed to multiple seasons even if you don't know for sure you're going to get multiple seasons. On the other side, though, like I said, it's a cast-driven medium. We *were* the show. Maybe they could afford to replace one of us, but not all of us. It wouldn't be the same show. Together we figured out we had some negotiating power if we worked as a unit. After season two, we all got together and decided we needed to say something and we needed to negotiate as a group. Because the initial offer for season three was a pittance. I'm not going to lie. It was four figures an episode. Which is nothing. Each season, they invest more and more in the show, so they increase the overall budget, allowing you to shoot more episodes. Season three was going to be fourteen episodes plus two reunion episodes. So, sixteen total. Which is a full run. That kind of told us how big we really were in terms of getting eyeballs on us. And eyeballs equal dollars. So, we wanted our fair share at that point.

At the same time, even though you know you have some bargaining power, they're still trying to instill the fear of God, death, taxes, and everything unholy in us, to get us to sign. They were saying, if we couldn't come to a consensus quickly, we wouldn't have the time we needed to shoot and get the show ready for the next year. So, we were up against that, too. At the end of the day, it all worked out. We agreed to a favored nations contract and our per episode salary went up something like six or seven times what it was previously. We went from four digits per episode to five for the season. So that was a nice bump. And we weren't shooting confessionals in broom closets anymore, so that was a bonus, too.

CHAPTER 12

THE REALITY OF IT ALL

Reality TV is not scripted any more than your own personal life is scripted. However, the editing process can be like scripting in reverse. It is manufactured in that way. The sequence of events might not be exact. Sections of conversation get cut out, so you end up with a kind of shorthand for what actually happened. But the emotions behind the drama, the humor, the revelations, that's all playing out in real time and it's mostly authentic. For instance, if you watch season one, there's a moment where I learn that my grandmother, my dad's mom, didn't hate me because I was gay. (Remember, she's the one that cursed me out and wanted nothing to do with me when I was a kid.) I knew she was an ornery old bag. I knew she didn't accept my mother because she was Muslim, and that's why when I was a kid she didn't warm up to me. After I was grown, though, she was still treating me like a second-class citizen. So, I assumed at that point, it must have been because I was gay. Turns out that wasn't the case. She hated me because I wasn't 100 percent Jewish. I found out on camera, and that reaction was real. I couldn't believe that was the thing. I'm half-Jewish, but that wasn't enough for her. It was mind-boggling to me. What's weird is I was so accustomed to homophobia, I'd accepted that it must have been that, and I was at peace with it. To find out she was okay with that, but not okay with me being half-Muslim, I couldn't even wrap my head around it. My grandmother legitimately did not love me for that reason.

I knew for certain that my real life would bleed into the show. What I wasn't prepared for was fame. Fame is when the *show* bleeds into your *real life*. Like I said, this was a small business when it started. We're talking six episodes. That's six hours minus commercial time. Six hours, but it's enough to be recognized. We were only shooting three months out of the year and not even getting the price of a good hand job for our trouble. The show itself wasn't a huge infringement on the everyday, but the reaction from the public was immediate once it aired. Remember, I was still working full time as a real estate agent. That wasn't staged; that was my life. Some strange shit started happening, and you know me always walking around with my guard up, I got really paranoid. And it was for good reason. Just because you're paranoid, doesn't mean they're not after you, right? I started having to vet every caller.

One time, right after the first season aired, I picked up the phone and a lady on the other end started with, "Hi, are you Reza?"

"Yes, I am," I said. "How may I help you?"

I shit you not, she goes, "I'm looking to buy a mansion."

First of all, I've sold a lot of real estate and a lot of homes that many would consider mansions. No one refers to a house they're looking to buy as a "mansion" unless they've won the lottery and could not otherwise afford a damn mansion. The red flag went full mast. But what do I know? Maybe this girl *did* win the lottery. So, I have my normal conversation. I ask for her name and a few other details, so I can google her while we're still on the phone. Sure enough, she's a stripper, and she's got a rap sheet. Yes, you can find that stuff out fast if you know what you're doing. She was not a lottery winner. She wasn't looking to drop cash on a mansion. She wanted to hang out. Sorry, ma'am, but no, I'm not going to come pick you up and take you around and show you homes. I do my research. Have you had your head checked recently?

It didn't always work, though. People can be sly as all hell. I got ambushed once. Totally swindled, and I'll never let myself live it down. My normally acute radar failed me. I got a phone call from this couple claiming to be a family in Beverly Hills who wanted me to sell their home for them. Yes, you could call it a mansion. They didn't. They gave me their names and address. I looked them up. It was their house. There was a clear record of ownership. They'd owned it for a really long time. They really sounded like they knew what they were talking about. They wanted me to put together some comps to gauge the asking price. They wanted me to put together an entire marketing strategy. It sounded front-to-back legit. It would be a big payday, and you know I was already thinking about my wardrobe for season two. I needed to spruce up the game, plan some outfits for the confessionals. I was in. I did all the work, like I would for anyone else. I gathered the comp details. I put together the strategy. I even got threads pressed at the dry cleaner. The mustache was trimmed. I was crisp. I went in looking like a million bucks.

On the day of the meeting, as I pulled onto their street, I could instantly see there were cars lined up on both sides of the street. It was packed. Like overflow festival parking. Naturally, I assumed someone on the block was having a party. I could hear music bumping as I was rolling up, and lo and behold, it was coming from the house where I was supposed to have this listing appointment.

At this point, I'm thinking, *Did they forget? Am I going to have to reschedule?* That's not totally out of the ordinary. The front door was open, so I walked in and a whole gang of kids rushed me. They were so excited to see me. It was like I was the clown showing up to make balloon animals or something. Turns out, the whole thing was a ruse. These people threw a damn party and conned me into coming so everyone could meet me. Equal parts flattering and terrifying. I've seen too many horror movies to think there was no way it could turn bad. But it didn't. Turns out they were actually fans, and this was their way of getting to meet me. They had about forty people there. I ended up taking a few pictures with everyone and laughing about it. It was like the Reza show. It was pretty hysterical. Even though I'd wasted a lot of time prepping for this meeting, because these people had no intention of selling their house.

I didn't feel like a celebrity, though. It felt more like I'd won a regional pie-eating contest at the county fair and people wanted a souvenir picture with me. Celebrity is a different feeling for me. I didn't understand the distinction until I started getting recognized by other celebrities. I remember the first time it happened. I was at what I think was a *Us Weekly* party. Lindsay Lohan was there, who, of course, I recognized. She had watched the show and seen my dad's family portrayed as from Long Island, so naturally, she assumed I had originally been from there as well. Long Island is where she is from. She came over and struck up a conversation with me, and we ended up chatting for quite a bit. Then this publicity photo floated out into the ether of the two of us chatting at that party. Seeing that felt different from being stalked by strippers at thc Keller Williams office. I have to admit, I loved it. I can see where it would be intoxicating for some people. Shortly after I enjoyed the experience, I was immediately wary of it. Again, I always have my guard up, and whenever something makes me feel flattered, I narrow my eyes. It turns into a "who wants me to feel like this, and what do they want out of me" sort of thing. It made me uncomfortable. I wasn't like Mike. I remember that time, when this all was first starting to happen. I'd look over at Mike and he'd be chugging a hydro flask full of his own Kool-Aid. Fully intoxicated. Will work for photo ops. He wore it like a seventies Jersey pimp's fox coat.

Honestly, even if I wanted to let myself go there, I couldn't. I had my mom, who's a very humbling bitch, to remind me at all times I wasn't above it all. She was like that the whole way through, too. But even before that, it's in her nature to always put me in check. Before I met Adam, I'd gone on this blind date at the Coral Tree Café with a Persian doctor. I showed up, and the guy was wearing True Religion jeans with the big white stitching and a Western-style embroidered shirt. He might as well have wrapped himself in red flags for a date with me. That's not my thing. And I could smell his cologne from across the restaurant. Imagine a room full of people eating delicious food, and it all tastes like this guy's cologne because that's all anyone can smell.

It was putrid. Then I sit down and start talking to him, and he has this thick accent. I was like, "How long have you been in the States?" It was like eight years. Eight years and he sounds like he got here last Thursday. That's definitely not my kind of vibe. It felt forced and inauthentic, so I couldn't deal. It felt like I was out on a date with my uncle, honestly. Not for me at all.

My mom, who must have been home waiting for her timer to go off, called immediately afterward. She was super excited because I was going out with a Persian Muslim doctor. Total hat trick for her. She tried to play it off, but I knew she was fishing for a positive response. She asked, in Farsi, "How was the date?" I told her straight. He was kind of jerky. He had a really big accent. I didn't like his outfit. He wreaked of cologne. I told her it was burn-your-nose bad. Not too much of it, but it was a cheap cologne to begin with. She said, "He's a doctor, though. Right?"

I'm like, "Yeah."

"What about you? You sell houses. Do the doctor." That's the kind of mom she is, always really good at keeping me very grounded and very levelheaded. I never liked the fame for its own sake. I did like, though, that it was giving me a platform and giving me a chance to have my say and be heard.

I did Soledad O'Brien's show after season one aired. Doing that was thrilling to me. Going into it, I couldn't wait. I knew they had assembled a panel of young gay people who were going to come at me for being a negative influence and reinforcing stereotypes about being gay and about being Persian. I was ready for them. They started coming after me and I unloaded. "You don't even know what you're looking at, with your penny loafers and your Oxford shirts." How can a Caucasian look at me and tell me that I'm portraying the worst stereotypes of *my* culture? The worst stereotypes of my culture are on the nightly news. It's the bombing, the hijacking, the terrorism, the theocracy; those are the worst parts of our culture. I'm disgusted by those. I'll own loving gold Rollies and Gucci and Mercedes all day long. Go ahead and think whatever those things make you think about me. Don't for a second think I come from a long line of terrorists. I told them straight up, "Get the hell out of here. I'm on a reality show. There's been no portrayal of Iranian Americans on TV before, much less a gay one. This is who I am, and I am humanizing us. I grew up with people looking for horns on the top of my head, so shut the hell up. I'm gay. My family loves me. My friends respect me. And I'm showing young people out there that it does get better. Don't kill yourself in those difficult years."

I hope that's still a big part of my legacy, and that this book is a part of that, too. If you're reading this right now and you're struggling with how society or your family sees you or is treating you, remember there's hope. We all go through it. I got through it. If I could get through it, y'all can, too.

CHAPTER 13

THE TELEVISION OF IT ALL

People on reality TV have fully four-dimensional lives, but then they're tethered to this TV show, too. You have a partner. You have a family. You have a business you're trying to run. Then someone from the network interrupts you while you're walking the dog before bed to give you your shooting schedule for the next day. This can happen really late at night, so then you have to scramble to rearrange the rest of your life around the shoot. As much as you appreciate being on the show, it can be really irritating when you're trying to go to the gym before you go meet a new client who wants you to sell their house.

But you do it. You reorder your whole life around this tight shooting schedule. You show up on time, then have to sit there for two hours because someone else in the cast didn't handle their business, and they show up late. It's not hurry up and wait. It's hurry up and wait on this person you're about to have drinks with. Meanwhile, there's some green production assistant who doesn't know what they're doing. They were supposed to get something we don't have, so we end up waiting on them. By the time cameras are rolling, you're already hot at all this other nonsense going on behind the scenes, so naturally you bring that energy into whatever starts happening in front of the camera. Keep in mind, we're mostly all fire signs to start with. Piss us off, throw us into a room together, add alcohol, call action, and repeat.

Then as the show went along, these people who are your real-life friends are also your colleagues. You've built this really successful business together, but not everyone is pulling their own weight. It was like being in a band. So, then the personal conflicts you're airing on the show are being driven emotionally by the problems you have with those same people for what you see them bringing or not bringing to the band. Just like any project, inevitably certain people aren't going to be keeping up their end. Ahem, Mike.

Yes, Mike was the squirrel of the show. He was keeping all his nuts buried. All the drama, or at least most of it, that was going on in his real life—he was managing to keep it off of the show. Naturally, yours truly would get irritated with that. Not with Mike the person, but with Mike the coworker. As far as bringing his personal life into the storyline, he was very deceptive. Producers and cast would have to beat the truth out of him at times to get a hint of reality. I don't want to say that he's a compulsive liar when it came to the show. Some might. But he was definitely deceptive, while I'm out here bleeding for the camera. I'm airing all my personal stuff with my dad being a ho, his mom being a ho, my homosexuality, and me being a ho before Adam, like real emotionally challenging day-to-day struggles. I'm being funny and laughing, being brash and extroverted, but I'm also sincerely crying and being serious for the sake of the show.

How could I not start to feel entitled in a way, with all that going on? Why would I think it's okay for us all to get paid the same? Are you kidding? I keep bringing it every day, while this fool is showing up and asking me right before the cameras roll what we should be talking about in the next scene. Of course, then anything he would do after that would get under my skin. It became very easy to pop off at him, in light of that. So, while the emotion was real, there were times when what was driving the heat was different from what we were arguing over in a given scene.

Case in point: He started making T-shirts. And not just any T-shirts. They were *Shah*'s T-shirts, with my image on them, and he was selling them without my permission. Really, homie? I don't even sell T-shirts. I don't like that. I don't want my likeness on cheap T-shirts. I don't want that as part of my brand or my business. I had to send a cease-and-desist letter to get him to stop selling shirts without my permission. You know what his response was? He said, "Sue me. It'll be a good storyline." That was his idea of how to make the show interesting. There was an artifice to it. After a few seasons, I'd be looking at him off camera, and to me he looked shocked that he was still being allowed to be on television. Like he couldn't believe year after year, he hadn't been clipped yet. He knew he was faking it to a degree.

Don't underestimate the power of petty jealousy, either. We became like siblings. The network isn't your parents trying to keep everything even. They don't play that game. So, you watch a few episodes, and you start to think about your place on the show versus the others. You've got the stopwatch out. It's clear who's getting more screen time and more scenes. You're talking to each other to find out who's doing more press. I got to do *Watch What Happens Live* first, and I know that rubbed some folks the wrong way. I don't want you to read this and think the show was one big put-on; it wasn't even close to that. It's that the dynamic between the cast members was much more complex than what was being talked about in a given scene.

There's someone else I need to mention before we move on, as it relates to what was going on behind the scenes at *Shahs*: a producer who did everything he could to make sure the pot was stirred and that emotions ran hot. Under his watch, the permits and the lighting setups and the craft service were not about to go to waste. We were going to give the editors the material they needed to make a show that the audience couldn't turn away from even if their house was burning down around them. His name was Esteve Yaghoubrashtizadeh. Esteve is the Persian pronunciation of the name Steve. Persians do that with a number of English words. If they can't pronounce it naturally, they add "Eh" to the beginning and that's how they get through it. Esteve was a royal shit disturber and made no bones about insulting us, turning us against each other, pissing us off…you name it. And he would always do it via email. He wasn't one of the on-set guys. He was some douche, sitting on his high horse in a studio somewhere, like a sinister god, watching everything we shot, making notes, then sending emails to the cast that he knew, I'm sure, would get the kind of reaction he wanted. To make it worse, this asshole kept promising to show up at the next event, would say things like, "I can't wait to have a drink with you all at the pool party." Then week after week, the fool ghosted us. Then after the shoot was over, we'd get this email from him talking trash about everyone and telling us we needed to do better. Lucky for all of us, I saved some of those emails, and some of the cast's responses, because this stuff is gold. It kept getting worse as it went, too. Every email, he'd be more of a dick than the last. He was sexist, racist, homophobic, and downright personally insulting. If I could cancel anybody, it would be his dumbass. The animosity we were starting to show toward him was very real. After a while, we hated him and couldn't wait for an opportunity to knock his ass out.

To give you a taste of the kind of crap he pulled via Gmail, check this out. He sent these to the entire original cast of season one. If you don't recognize a couple of the names, meaning if you were late to the party or plain don't remember, this included all the aforementioned as well as Anita Gohari and David Golshan. This is from July 22, 2011. We'd been shooting for a few days, but we had a big party coming up on July 24 that we were all aware of. As a lead-in to that party, this dude we'd never met and don't know, who has already been sending some mildly offensive shit, offers up this gem:

So, I heard that the checks are in the mail. Maybe some of you should use some… I mean, all of that money to upgrade the wardrobe. Showing up and looking like you raided the lost and found at the Kabobi is not okay! This is Bravo people… Step it up.

I'm looking forward to throwing a few back tomorrow!

Shabbot Shalom,
Esteve

Seriously, dude, WTF? You don't throw your cast under the bus like that, right? We were all pissed but intimidated at the same time. We didn't know how much power this guy had. One false move, and we could end up on the cutting room floor or worse. Mike, at the very least, defended us in the thread. But you can see from his tone and my subsequent confusion, this is already landing wrong with everyone. Mike wrote this:

> *Shahs...*
>
> *Please do not even waste your precious energy or time worrying about these bullshit, cheap, and tasteless emails.*
>
> *As Katt Williams so cleverly said:*
>
> *"If you need someone to hate on hate on me...tell me my hair ain't luxurious bitch when u know it is."*

Then I chimed in, responding to Mike, wondering who the hell this dude was:

> *What if Esteve is a ninth castmate and we're meeting his ass tomorrow?*

Turns out I was wrong. Esteve never showed up. The party

turned into a cast party. So, it was only us in front of the cameras. Everyone had a great time, but before we can even go to bed for the night, Esteve, who was apparently spying on us, sent this:

Tonight went well.

I think that everyone looked decent, and by decent, I mean you didn't look like you should have been working at the restaurant instead of patronizing it. Some of you drank too much, while others ate too much... You know who you are. Let's try to keep this classy, we're representing Iranians as a whole, we don't want to come across as trashy, ENOUGH WITH THE RELIGIOUS SHIT! *Have respect for one another, and don't eat and drink so much because it's free... Someone still ends up paying for it, in more ways than one.*

David was doing the funky chicken. Mike was taking/making calls. Reza ate all the dessert, and if his shirt was buttoned any lower, that gold amulet would have been on the table. Golnesa wasn't engaging in as much dialog as had been expected, and Asa was looking more like the rest of the cast, didn't see that coming. Sammy, well Sammy was Sammy PC to the end. MJ looked like she had the best time, and Anita looked good enough to eat.

I was hoping to see you tonight, but at the last minute, changes were made, and it became a cast-only party. Hopefully I'll see you all at Sammy's pool party.

Sleep well,
Esteve

Okay, it's not the worst thing in the world, right? It's mildly insulting considering you're sending an email to a bunch of strangers who are newly getting their feet wet in the medium and are putting themselves out there for the first time. The comments about the food and the eating. Making fun of the way I dress. Telling Anita she looked good enough to eat is unprofessional and aggressive. Singling her out in a room full of other women you criticized is not kind at best. I probably wouldn't be bringing him up if it had stopped there. It didn't stop there, of course. In the lead-up to Sammy's pool party, which he mentioned in the previous email, he sent this... And this is where he really started to cross the line with us:

"Some are hot, some are not."—Ryan Seacrest, about the cast. What category will you fall into at the pool party?

Is Reza going to wear a speedo? Gays love those, but hoping NOT! Is MJ gonna be serving those DDD boobs as the main course, now that I want to see. Is David SOOOOO OOOOOOOOOOOOOOOOOOOOOOOOOOOOOO OOOOOOOO excited to finally have a reason to be shirtless on camera? YOU KNOW it! Hopefully he won't be bringing the uglies with him. And papa Sammy, will you be sitting on a throne not lifting a finger? Are you gonna wear a speedo? Maybe Reza can loan you one. TWINS!

How many girls will Mike kiss? Better yet, how many girls will he &$#@%!

GG and Anita TINY TINY TINY bikinis please… YUM! Asa, one piece please (and don't forget to wax)!

See you on Saturday!

Yours comfortably,
Esteve Joon

Yours comfortably? Who is this clown? How the hell is this even remotely cool? This isn't merely unprofessional, it's straight up offensive to anyone who reads it. This dude is quoting Seacrest basically shaming part of the cast for not being hot enough for TV. Once again, though, our own Golnesa, never one to back down from a fight, had had enough. She put a nail through his forehead with some choice words of her own. Love you for this, GG, replying to Esteve:

You're such a pathetic piece of shit. The good thing is that now I do know who you are and I will come after your fat, nappy, ugly whore ass as soon as the cameras are done. You will look deformed by season two. Keep it up bitch. Just one question... Why is your mom such a nasty whore to make you into a nasty whore? I guess it's true that the apple doesn't fall far from the tree. See you soon.

Yours affably,
Golnesa G.

"Yours affably." HA! Turning his own sarcastic sign-offs back at him. The only problem is Golnesa was bluffing. She did not know who he was. Esteve's identity would remain a mystery until he was satisfied with how the cast was performing in front of the camera. After all, if you're going to get the kind of content that will set America on fire, as a good producer, you have to stoke the emotional flames so to speak. Who cares if they're pissed at the man behind the curtain, so long as they take it out on each other, right?

At least that was my thinking when I invented Esteve, this phony producer persona, created a Gmail account for him, and decided it would be really fun to torment my fellow castmates. *Come on, now. You know I love a good prank.* Especially one that makes for even better television. And doubly true if it's the show I'm on. You didn't think a real television producer would get away with saying the kind of vile bile I was spilling, did you? I had to include shots at myself, of course, to make sure I didn't rouse any suspicion. All the while biting my lip whenever we'd sit around pre-shoot and trade theories about who this asshole Esteve was. I played along, chipping in my own theories. Meanwhile, by the time the director yelled, "Cameras up!" Blood was boiling. And I loved every minute it of it. That's my sense of humor. Like the time I smuggled a spray bottle of Liquid Ass—a prank fart spray—onto our Sprinter van and blew up the onboard bathroom with it. I had everyone gagging, thinking someone had actually gone in there and knowingly unloaded on us all instead of asking politely for a stop at the gas station. Nothing beats watching your friends fret and point fingers, when you and only you know you're the real culprit and that the whole thing was done for the sake of a good laugh. BTW, if you are not familiar with Liquid Ass, I highly recommend you invest in a small bottle from Amazon. I get no kickbacks, I assure you. I'm not the CEO or an investor. But the next time you're at a friend's house or at your parents' place, sneak off to the toilet, unload a couple of spritzes, then sit back and wait. I promise you a night of disgust and laughter you will never forget.

CHAPTER 14

BEST IN SHOW

Aside from the show itself being a transformative experience, many of the life events chronicled on Bravo were transformative in their own right. For better or worse, my proudest and most regretful moments over the past decade can be purchased on Amazon Prime for a buck ninety-nine per episode. To what degree did being on the show play a role in how those big life moments played out? I don't know. I know that if there had been no cameras running, no production, no press, they would have played out differently, but they would have been no less important to me.

One of the most important moments for me in my personal life, something I am so proud of still, is the moment I became a naturalized American citizen. This happened well before *Shahs*, you can't buy or rent it, but it meant a lot to me. What you can see on the show is a dispute I got into back in 2017 with GG and Shervin, when I wanted the group to take a trip to Israel. This was something very near and dear to my heart as the son of a Jewish father. Of course, the more Muslim-leaning members of the cast were less enthused and worried that they might be met with a less-than-warm welcome. In trying to get everyone on board, when they brought up the conflict between Iran and Israel, I said, "Fuck Iran." Yes, I'm Persian, and yes, I said this to a lot of Persians. I'm not surprised they reacted negatively. I am a bit surprised they didn't understand where I was coming from when I said it. I stand by it. There was a ton of backlash from that moment online. People were coming after me. GG and Shervin got pissed at me. I don't care. Like I explained to Andy on *Watch What Happens Live*. Loosely paraphrasing, I told Andy: I'm gay. Do you know what they do to homosexuals in Iran? Or to anyone who has a different religion, or alternate lifestyle, or even a different opinion from the government in that country? They murder you. They hang you. They stone you. They behead you. They beat you with a whip in the public square. When I said F Iran, I was talking about the regime, the government, the religious dictatorship. If you have not lived outside of America, if you were blessed to be born a citizen of this incredible country, and you are criticizing me for condemning the country I was born in, you might be taking your own freedom for granted. I don't know what the United States means to you, but to me it means I'm free to be alive. If I were forced to grow up in Iran, I would be dead now. They would have killed me. I am alive today because I am an American citizen. Period. End of discussion. The next time you're planning out the barbecue menu for your Fourth of July party, or planting a tiny flag in your planter to celebrate that day, take a moment to appreciate it from the point of view of an immigrant like me. We aren't here because we hate this country. We're here because we love it. We're here because it might be the only safe place in the world for us to be. Freedom isn't a given. I've called my U.S. citizenship the greatest gift I've ever received, and I mean that. Before that happened, I still had an Iranian passport. I hadn't lived there since I was three years old, but it still said, "Issued by the Islamic Republic of Iran." Try getting through security at the airport with that post-9/11.

I had tears in my eyes at my swearing-in ceremony. Remember I had nightmares when I was a kid that I wouldn't get to stay here. Being able to say, "I'm a U.S. citizen," means something incredibly special to me. I get to walk where I want, think what I want, feel how I want, and say what I want. I get to be who I authentically am as a human being without fear of reprisal outside X. Becoming an American means gaining your independence, remember that. I've been blessed to travel freely all over this country. I feel safe and accepted just about everywhere I've been. It's not like I can hide my national origin, either. I look very Middle Eastern, I have a very Middle Eastern–sounding name. And it is a testament to this country and the culture it can foster, that many years later, looking back at all the vitriol and suspicion cast at Persian immigrants when we first got here, that's mostly evaporated at this point. I'd like to think that *Shahs* and my role in it played a big part in changing that perception of Persians.

My desire, from a very young age, to be a shah came to fruition on TV. Like I said, I idolized the Shah. I admired everything he represented. By the time I actually got to take the title, what I wanted to represent and accomplish as a shah had changed. I wanted to reframe the entire concept of what it meant to be from the Middle East for Americans. Imagine me, a funny pro-American gay Iranian living the good life in Beverly Hills making people laugh in living rooms all over the country. That's what I was envisioning. Talk about outside the box. How the hell was that going to work?

Well, it did.

I cannot tell you how incredible it feels every time someone reaches out to me on X or Instagram or wherever to let me know that I made a positive impact in their life. It's still hard for me to connect with other people on my Americanness. Call it patriotism. Call it an appreciation of liberty. People are shocked by the way I approach this subject. They judge a book by its cover. I hope more and more the people following me on social media and other platforms or reading this book will understand I share their strong sense of patriotism for the United States because of the personal liberty it affords all of its citizens. Is homosexuality welcome in every circle? No. Are homosexuals being hung from cranes by the government for the sin of being born? No. Exactly. People need to stop comparing this country to a nonexistent utopia and see it in the context of the other countries in the world where personal liberty is not a cultural value.

Here's the other thing, though, when it comes to my love of this country and my patriotism and the incredible nostalgia I feel when I think back to that day that I took the oath, was sworn in, and made my citizenship official. Even after that day, for a very long time, I always felt somewhere in my bones that I was a Persian living in America. I was born somewhere else. That place I came from is still out there. I am still tied to it and it to me in this toxic relationship. That all changed while the cameras were rolling, and it's probably the most positively impactful moment for me in the entire run of the show.

It was in season three, episodes twelve and thirteen, "Return to the Homeland Parts One and Two." If you have been touched by the emotional journey in this book and would like to watch this particular experience unfold in real time, I invite you to do so. It brought me to tears and was a major turning point in my life. This was not something manufactured for the cameras. This was something Asa and I experienced together. She arranged the entire experience for us. She got us transportation where they were going to sneak us to the Turkish–Iranian border, to get us as close as possible to Iran. I'm like, "Sneak us to the border?" I didn't understand. We weren't actually going to be in Iran. Why are we sneaking? Here I was, this California boy who had traveled to Mexico many, many times. All over Mexico actually, but including popping over the border into Tijuana. There's this little stamping in the ground, one side saying "Mexico," the other "United States." There are gift shops and currency exchanges, and you can actually walk across the border, if you want to fly to, say, Puerto Vallarta, and not pay to fly out of San Diego. You can walk across the border legally into the airport in Mexico and fly to Puerto Vallarta from there because the flights are so much cheaper. Pro tip: If you live in SoCal and want to visit someplace in Mexico other than Tijuana, fly out of Mexico. So, when they initially suggested going to the border of Iran, I thought it was going to be like that. Like I could buy a snow globe full of sand at the gift shop. I don't know what I was thinking.

Anyway, we flew to Istanbul. Then from Istanbul we flew to Van, Turkey, which is a border town. Once we got to Van, we had a guide and security detail. I'm talking full-on armed guards. They took us by car to a Bedouin village. And then from there, we got into these dune buggies. We weren't just off-road; we were off the map. It was terrifying. We were going full speed over what were basically giant piles of rocks. It was seriously like the Indiana Jones Adventure at Disneyland. Asa and her mom and I were being thrown into each other in the back of this thing. We're so far off-road, you can't *see* the road. I didn't know where the hell we were. If we were going to be sold into the black market or held for ransom. It was freakin' sketch. So trepidatiously I asked the guide where we were going and why we had to go over all these damn rocks and shit to get there. He told me, and this was the moment my butt really started to pucker, he said, "We want to stay out of AK-47 range, because if they can see you, they can shoot you." Seriously, dude? Did he reference not only an assault rifle, but a specific make and model? He then relayed this whole story where, on the Armenian side of the border with Iran, a shepherd's dog had pulled free and crossed the border into Iran. The shepherd chased the dog in and he'd been shot and killed. They were seriously driving us over these boulders because they wanted to keep us from being spotted so we didn't get shot. Mind you, out in the middle of nowhere, dune buggies make a whole hell of a lot of noise. And it's the only thing you can hear for miles. I'm like, "Bro, are we out of earshot, too?"

The dune buggies got us to this other Bedouin village—we're talking really remote now, where the elder of the village wanted a Snickers bar from America to give us safe passage. Seriously. There was a certain amount of money, too, but what he really wanted was a Snickers. They had made those arrangements with him prior to our arrival, we came prepared with Snickers, and that's why they let us pass. We didn't hang around to watch him eat it. Though, I can imagine the pleasure he must have felt biting into that candy bar. Again, America, appreciate yourself.

From that village we went by truck into the hills, and then we stopped. The engines were cut. We stepped out and ascended on foot a short distance further, maybe fifty yards, when the guard pointed out over the land in front of us and said, "There it is." There it was. Iran. The place I was born. I hadn't laid eyes on it since before my long-term memories had started to form. That place in the photographs and the stories. The place where the sounds, tastes, and smells of my parents' house had come from. A place I loved for what it was. A place that now hated me for what I was. Asa, myself, and Asa's mother were the only three who'd made the journey. We were all in tears. And this is the only time I've ever experienced this, but it was both a happy and a sad cry all at once. We were happy because we'd come so far to see the land that had given rise to us. We were breathing

Iranian air. Asa mused that the wind was blowing toward us, so the clouds that were over Iran would soon be over us. We were sad, too, that as close as we were, it was as close as we'd ever be able to get. The members of our family who lived on that foreign land would always be foreign to us. We'd never be able to see them again. Aunts, uncles, cousins, all lost to history and religious conflict.

Leading up to this moment, I really hadn't been able to anticipate how it was going to make me feel. I had to be there. Being there I realized there was nothing there for me on the other side of that border. It rang true, finally. The journey to get to that point had been the catharsis I was looking for all along. I'd lived my whole life with nothing but anger and resentment for that country. Iran and everything the Ayatollah stood for had made me feel bad about where I came from. Seeing Iran with my own eyes, my own history came into focus, and I understood how much time and energy I had wasted having emotions about this place that doesn't give a damn about me. Iran doesn't care how I feel about it. Iran was nothing more than a shitty abusive ex. And the feelings all ended there. From the time I'd landed at the airport, throughout the entire journey to get to this point, I'd slowly been releasing and diffusing those emotions. Draining them from my being as if all I'd ever need to feel this release was to take this journey I'd completed. Now I could stand there looking at this place and feel nothing for it. I was not them. They are not me. I don't represent them. They don't represent me.

The reassurance that I needed had already come from the travel guide. He had no idea of his impact on me, I assure you of that. But he had been the catalyst for the change in my heart and my soul that I needed. It came when we were in the dune buggies, and I asked him why he had gone to all this extent to keep us safe, and he said so you won't get shot. I said something about not even being on Iranian soil and wondered why they would want to shoot me. And he said, "Because you're American, brother." That was the moment. I was like, *Damn straight. I am a motherf!$#ing American.* I'm American, and I'm going home. And your boy went home a new man.

We had an amazing trip. A once-in-a-lifetime reclamation of our spirits. As we traveled back to Istanbul, I could feel a fundamental shift in how I saw myself well up and wash over me. That day, I made real peace with the idea that I am not where I come from. It was crazy to be that close to them and realize they hate me. This profound, life-changing experience helped me come to terms with how tribal the society I came from really was and is. The tribal norms taught are that your actions reflect upon your family. If you get a divorce, they treat it like it's a disease. The catty whispers in the corner. "Ooh, you don't want to marry into that family. Divorce runs in that family." It's the same way with being gay or poor or anything else that's outside the norm. They act like it is toxic and should be treated like illness. We're taught that how we behave trickles down on the tribe that we're from. And Persian Americans see themselves as one big tribe, all centered around this country we were born in that means nothing. Here I am, on a TV show, and I've had these angry Persians telling me I'm not a good representation of them. All of those years, that whole backlash, led up to this moment, too. Meanwhile, I don't give a damn, because I had all my own animosity and anger toward that country for all the young gay people being stoned to death, alongside all the other humanitarian atrocities that are committed there. Women are second-class citizens and all that. That was a lot to carry. Then this tour guide with one sentence put it all in perspective and gave me a pardon for all of it. "You're American." I really needed to hear that, and I didn't know how bad I needed to hear it. I had no idea it was even possible to break free from those chains of generational trauma. But here I was, unshackled. I felt like the casino dealer at the craps table during shift change. Like I clapped my hands together to prove I wasn't taking anything with me, and it was all good. We'd cried. Then we turned around, and we laughed and hugged and we left. It was something else. On our way out, we saw signs, street signs with arrows pointing the opposite direction from the way we were going, that said "Iran." That said it all. It was like shedding a thousand pounds of shame that I had been carrying around for the hostage crisis and everything after that. Remember, all the low-down dirty things Iran had done, whether it was funding Hamas or Hezbollah or saying "Death to America," being part of the Axis of Evil. They're still doing it, dude. The fight goes on for basic human rights and dignity. Do we need to get another announcement from another president? Whatever it's going to take to kick the theocrats out and get that place out of the dark ages, I'm all for it. I'll be on the sideline cheering and dropping into the Ayatollah's DMs to tell him how much I'm looking forward to the day he hangs from a crane. Seriously, F that guy and everything he stands for.

At this point, to me, Iran is a place I visited. I have dope pictures from there. I took a rock from that hillside and gave it to MJ. It was shaped like a heart.

CHAPTER 15

CANCELED CULTURE

Here's what you should understand about being a "reality TV personality": That's exactly what you are. In town, they don't call it "reality TV," because it's not a good reflection of reality. They call it "unscripted." It's a TV show you shoot without a script. They don't give you dialogue. There's no rehearsal. We aren't actors. We're personalities let loose in a preconceived scenario. We aren't improvisational TV, because improv relies on performers creating characters as they go. It's kind of like that, except you aren't creating a character, you're acting out your own personality and bringing your real-life conflicts and emotions to play. We literally wound ourselves up like toys, and when they called action, we let ourselves go. We were only trying to be our genuine selves and live our actual lives without acknowledging the show aspect of it. When we first started, we thought, *They're going to put our real lives on TV.* The way that the producers talk to you, that's what they make it seem like. This is life. This isn't a show. It's all real. None of it is fake. Before you know it, though, you're addicted to the vibe, and you more than ride it, you *drive* it. Between seasons you have nothing to do but wait and think about what you'll do if you get another season. What clothes do you want to wear in the confessional? What relationships or personal issues are you're dealing with that you think would make for good television? How can you approach those on camera? You can't help but get caught up in what I experienced as a hamster-wheel effect, where you're compulsively running in place and fueling this conveyor belt of personal excitement and anxiety with the effort. You shoot a season. You wait with bated breath for it to air. Then you chomp your nails waiting to know what the ratings were. Then you spin in circles waiting to find out if you're getting picked up for another season or not. Then you learn that you're getting another season and all that pre-thought and shopping you put into it is actually going to get a chance to hit the stage. You find out you got a bigger episode commitment. You fight and claw to get a little bigger piece of the pie.

Also, now you've had a chance to develop the relationships with your castmates both on-screen and off, so those dynamics start to change in the offseason when the cameras aren't rolling.

You start thinking about how you're going to handle certain people and their situations that you know they're dealing with. You start to think about how you're going to come across in the editing room. What sound bite do you want them to use, for instance, when you are confronting a certain castmate about something they did or said that pissed you off. You can't help it. You're not scripting anything, but you're definitely plotting.

You do that from season one to two. Season two to three. Season three to four. And every step along the way, the budget goes up. Your cut of the budget goes up. Your level of celebrity goes up. The stakes get higher and higher. The anxiety and excitement doubles and triples. It's an absolute roller-coaster ride. High highs and low lows. At first, you want people to pay attention, but then people start to become followers or fans or haters. Seriously, people you've never met and never will meet start to like you or dislike you. They compliment you publicly. They attack you publicly. Everything you say and do is being judged in the court of public opinion. You're looking over your shoulder for the shame lady from *Game of Thrones* and her bell. Seriously, you wake up in a cold sweat because you can hear that shit ringing in your sleep. You can be deafened and blinded by all the feedback. People have strong, sometimes toxic, opinions about how you look, what you wear, your family, your lifestyle, and everything in between.

Going back to the kind of roles we all play in our lives, viewers start to question how you play all those roles. They ask, "What kind of brother is he? What kind of husband is he? What kind of friend is he? What kind of son is he?" It's a bottomless pit of opinion. So, you're under all that scrutiny, but then the cameras turn off and you actually have to go home and *be* a good husband, a good son, a good friend, a successful salesman. And you have to do all of that, you have to be high functioning, after everything you've read about yourself and heard yelled at you is built up inside of you. That was one piece I didn't expect. When I was planning out my master plan of bringing acceptance and understanding and enthusiasm for Persians, I thought I had to learn how to function as a reality TV personality. And I felt like I was up to that challenge, and I think I can honestly say I was. The challenge I didn't know I needed to worry about was how hard it would be to go back into my normal everyday routine and still function once I was successful and a recognizable personality people liked. I didn't know how to navigate that. There were all kinds of ramifications I didn't anticipate. It really did make being off camera harder than being on camera at times. On television, the biggest concern was to get to the next season. In real life, the drama can hurt your mama, for real.

How did I balance it? I really don't know. To be totally honest, I don't know how many people could have done it for ten years without cracking. I think it must take a special makeup for it to not totally mess you up from head to toe, inside and out. It can. It does. It's really intense.

Then one day, it's all over. It took two years to get the ball rolling. It took a minute for it to stop in its tracks. One minute, you're lying on the beach after nine successful seasons. Your ratings are still high. You're taking season ten for granted, which maybe was my cardinal karmic error. The next minute you're being told you're not being brought back. The reason? No reason. It's just over. It's someone else's turn. It wasn't even done in person but over a short video conference with producers and the cast. No argument to be made. No appeal to be had. "Was it something I said?" No. "But what if we..." Nope. Nada. Only a dial tone. Or whatever the modern equivalent is. A blinking cursor, maybe?

Talk about emotional bloodletting. When I got off that call, I didn't know if I'd be able to stand up. I was disoriented to the point of being dizzy. The computer screen in front of me, now a screensaver, was ebbing in and out of focus. I started getting nauseous in the way you do from motion sickness after you get off your ninth roller coaster of the day at Six Flags. I got a headache. And the world was quiet. I couldn't hear the hum of the air conditioner or the buzz of a housefly. There was nothing but a sudden sensory void I'd never experienced before. The screen went dark, and I could see my reflection, and I thought, *Who am I?* My identity had become so intertwined with being a Bravolebrity. My thoughts and activities and aspirations were on that cycle. That hamster wheel. But now, I've been kicked off the wheel. The wheel is still spinning, but I'm not on it, when all the while, I thought the wheel needed me to keep running to rotate.

Nothing I'd prioritized in my life for the past decade meant anything in that moment. The fresh threads I had hanging in the closet for those confessionals, I could start the process of returning them. And there's no one to assist you, either. To reorient you or help you up off the ground. Those people who've been on your ass every day, making you the center of their world, scheduling your life, and planning their lives around that schedule, too—they don't give a damn about you anymore. In an instant, there's no relationship at all. No sentimentality. No legacy. No tears shed. It's as if none of it ever happened or mattered to them at all. You as a person don't matter to them. You were a cog in their machine, and they've replaced you with a shiny new cog.

How do you deal with that type of a breakup? Personally, I figured out how to cope as I went. It's not like there's a decompression chamber where they keep you for three days before allowing you to return to the surface. You're just there. You have to self-regulate. Adjusting back to what feels like civilian life is tough. I'm not saying I was on the front lines or anything that dramatic. I don't have PTSD from having been on television or anything like that. But there was a period where instead of acting out this heightened version of myself on a TV show, I was doing my acting at home. I was acting like everything was okay with me now that there was not a TV show. Meanwhile, inside I had these conflicting feelings. First I had feelings of gratitude that I was able to do something so special, and so near and dear to me, in the first place. But that was coupled with a profound sense of loss after it was gone. There was some anger and bitterness, too, about the way in which it ended. It felt so anticlimactic. For me, I wanted a conclusion to the story. Some sense of catharsis or full circle, but it wasn't there to be had.

A piece of me felt like it was dying. Not dying, like it had been murdered. Like my inner child was going to get his own dateline episode. *Shahs* was a huge part of my personal identity for a very long time. Hell, I'd always wanted to be a shah, and I'll be damned if I didn't get to be one. When I was on the show, I looked in the mirror and saw someone who was doing something awesome and unique. All that work and time I invested for over a decade brought me to this place where I had my own little kingdom. Then all of a sudden, the kingdom was lost. This beautiful palace I'd built around me was lifted off of the foundation by a helicopter and flown away. Now I was in an empty lot, and nobody could tell me why. They said, "It's business." Now get off our lot before we sic the dogs on you.

In a way, it's like losing any other job. You have to move on to the next and find a way to deal with everyday life. Real reality isn't gone. The cameras are. When my dad started to get really sick, when I could see his time was coming and when I found out that there had been this dementia he was dealing with for a long time, I very quickly realized not only is that all that matters, but that's all that's ever really mattered. The show, the celebrity, the money, that drive to hit those marks, all that energy has to be redirected or allowed to dissipate out into the universe, because you don't need that gear anymore. I shifted my focus to Dad, to Adam, to Mom. I started working on this book. I guess these pages are my way of having not an ending, but a chance to at least close this chapter the way I feel it needs to be closed. If not for the sake of the story, or for the audience, at least for me. There was no *Shahs* finale.

I didn't see it coming. I'd planned what I was going to say in episode one of season ten, but I hadn't given any thought as to what I would say if there was no season ten. The cancellation definitely affected me in a way I'm not proud of. I was mad at myself for being so stunned and soft when it happened. Mentally, every season before this one, I acted like all the prep I was doing for the next season would be a waste of time. I kept telling myself, *There's not going to be another season.* This time, though, I was thinking differently. I don't know why. Season ten seemed like such a lock; I let myself believe it was a done deal. I even got a text from one of the producers telling me they wouldn't be on season ten, but they'd be back for season eleven. Hello, that kinda thing inspires confidence, yo. If this guy is saying that, then there must be conversations I'm not privy to about it, right? So, whereas before, I'd never let my emotions get into the idea of a next season until it was a sure thing, this time I did. I let all my reservations go. I thought I was okay. I put myself on that high. And it made the drop all the more painful and my reaction all the more embarrassing. That's a big part of this for me. My reaction, because I was so hurt, to me was pathetic. I was so sad and so depressed, and I felt desperate. It hurt me in a way that I was not mentally and emotionally and spiritually prepared for.

It wasn't merely how cold the producers and studio were about it, either. The way my castmates were acting around the demise of it was surreal, too. I was so dedicated to this show for so long; why were they not being affected the way I was? It made me feel like I'd been in a psycho killer movie, not a reality show, and that everyone was a killer but me. Despite the fact that the feelings are valid, I still am critical of myself for feeling that way and reacting the way I did. I wish I'd been less orphan Oliver with his bowl, begging for more, more action hero walking away from a building as it explodes in the background.

I had a call with one of the executives a week after the canceling, and I went off a bit. I told her, straight up, "You guys suck. The ship went down on your watch." When we were with Ryan Seacrest Productions, we were really appreciated. We used to get Christmas presents with Christmas cards. It was heartfelt. And you could sense there was value for you as a person, not only a performer. I felt like I was more to them than a means to an end. Then when we switched production companies, everything changed. We stopped getting presents. We started getting cards. Then cards were basically a note that said they made a donation in your name to some random place. They didn't even bother to ask us what charity we preferred. It was totally impersonal. It felt like conveyor-belt relationship maintenance. Then we stopped getting that. And there was nothing. They basically rode the horse into the ground and shot it in the head when it ran out of steam. There was no reinvestment. No creative input. We didn't even ever get a new main title shoot. I looked completely different by season nine, but in the opening credits I still had jet black hair and the mustache. It was still the Halloween costume. I didn't look anything like that anymore. I let her know how I felt about the amount of commitment they didn't put into the show. It was the first time I had an opportunity to let someone know I felt about it.

I'm all better now. It took a few months, but by the end of the year, I was done. I'd given up hope that there was going to be some element of rekindling or reconciliation. I deleted the numbers of everyone who worked for the production company and the network. I stopped following Bravo- and Peacock-related Instagram posts. I didn't wanna see anything from them come up in my feed. It was a bad breakup. We've all had bad breakups. This was a bad breakup.

Ending any relationship is a transition. The person you are with can inform who you are in so many ways. How and when you eat, sleep, dress, whatever... When *Shahs* ended, I felt like a snake needing to shed its skin. The clothes that I used to wear on that show, I can never wear again. Like if I'd adopted my significant other's sports team and started wearing the jersey. I no longer support you, so I'm shitcanning the jersey, you know? Now it bothers me to support that team because I am no longer doing it to support that person. The jewelry I wore on that show, the Cartier LOVE bracelets and that Rolex I always had on, pretty much everything that went along with the version of Reza who was in a relationship with the show was a done deal as far as I was concerned. None of that was part of who I was going to be moving forward. I didn't want to look like that because of how it made me feel. I was ready to call Sotheby's or Christie's and give them all of those relics that I don't want as a part of my present or future anymore.

To me, all of that wardrobe and all those accessories were like my cape and my crown. I got to wear it. I got to be the Shah. Now, though, just like the Shah being exiled from his country, I needed to leave behind the things no longer relevant to where I was going. What's the point of being a king without a country? Don't think I felt like that out of bitterness. Not at all. It came from me asking myself, "Do I really want to walk around still dressing like the king when I know damn well the monarchy has been dissolved?" How ridiculous does that sound? Imagine Mohammad Reza Shah with the crown, the cape, and the scepter roaming around the East Village as if the revolution never happened. When a baseball player retires, he doesn't keep wearing the uniform around town. He doesn't go tromping through Starbucks in his cleats. Hell no. Not me.

I took my cue instead from the Shah's wife. There's an incredible documentary called *From Tehran to Cairo*. It's available in its entirety on YouTube if you want to watch it. If you want to learn more about the Shah and the fall of Iran, I highly recommend you do. It's really amazing and touching. In it, Queen Farah Pahlavi, the Shah's wife, recounts her personal stories and talks through the experience of what it was like to be exiled in Cairo after the kingdom fell. This is a woman who lost two of her children to suicide. She lost her husband, the Shah, to cancer. She lost her entire country and had to flee while many of her countrymen were chanting for her death for many, many years. At one point, the interviewer asks her about all of the jewelry, the adornments, and specifically, her crown. They ask what she did with all of that when she knew she was going to be forced to flee. Most of that stuff, she recounts, belonged to the government, so it wasn't like she could just take it with her. There was, though, one crown that the Shah had bought for her. It belonged to her. It was her crown. She says when she was leaving, one of the people around her told her to take that crown. She said, you know, if she left and was never able to come back, then she would never wear that crown again. All I'm saying is I'm that kind of queen.

My post-Shah journey, which includes writing this book, has been a long and emotional one to be sure. Adam and I spent this time readjusting. We converted our old house into a *Shahs*-themed Airbnb—look it up if you're ever in LA and want to have a real *Shahs* experience. We also built a guesthouse in our new house for my mom, so she can live with us as she gets older and less able to rely on herself. MJ and I remained in a good place, working on our relationship without cameras. We both wanted it so badly and it only got better and stronger as time passed. In telling my story in these pages, I found so much more compassion for my father, realizing that he was just a man, someone who had a whole entire life before I ever came along. I realized that

I am much more like him than I ever thought, and I'm proud of that now.

I also came to peace with the fact that my last "country" fell—I'm talking the TV show, not Iran. From March 11, 2012, the day the first episode of *Shahs* aired, to the day we were canceled, I lived with a weight in my chest. A weight that only got heavier with each passing moment. There was a prevalent anxiety throughout our entire run that, at any minute, the other shoe would drop. Someone would come out of the woodwork and falsely accuse me of something awful. Reza did this to me. Reza said that to me. And my world would come caving in around me. Some stranger, or worse, one of my castmates, God forbid, would have it in for me and start a rumor that would steamroll my life. That drama has become all too familiar in the age of unhinged social media, and it can be what shows like *Shahs* thrive or dive off from. It got so bad for me, I had to start taking antidepressants while we were filming *Shahs of Sunset*. I still take them, but I feel completely different now. I'm on the tiniest dose.

The perspective I gained from the separation with *Shahs* and the adoration that grew for how wonderful the experience was only added fuel to my fire. Something that had felt like a burden became an inspiration. No matter how much I'd like to say I didn't miss my old bad relationship, after *Shahs of Sunset* wrapped in 2021, I felt this void—not just for me, but for our fans who loved watching the messy, real, and hilarious moments with me, GG, and MJ. That show was our heart and soul for nine seasons, showcasing Persian culture, our friendships, and all the drama that came with it. When it ended, I knew we weren't done telling our stories. The love from the fans, the DMs, the comments—they kept us going, and I couldn't shake the feeling that we had more to share.

My already close relationships with both MJ and GG only grew in depth and mutual appreciation. So much so that MJ, GG, and I spent a considerable amount of time and energy devising a way to continue to tell our stories that felt empowering and rejuvenating. We asked ourselves, "How could we branch off from *Shahs* in a way that was genuine to who we'd become?" There were offers that didn't come through and ideas that never went anywhere. So goes show business. Despite the struggles and disappointments, the beat went on, we kept brainstorming, and we kept hope for a continuation on our terms alive.

Fast forward to 2024, and the universe started aligning. I was approached by Alex Baskin, the executive producer of *many* hit reality shows. His idea for us was simple but invigorating: Take the heart of *Shahs*—our culture, our bond, our unfiltered chaos—and mix it with the vibe of *The Valley*, that *Vanderpump Rules* spinoff that's all about navigating life's next chapter in the San Fernando Valley. I've always loved how *The Valley* captures real moments—marriage, kids, businesses—and Alex thought, why not bring our Persian flavor to that world? MJ, GG, and I couldn't agree more.

The spark for this show came from years of living, growing, and staying tight with GG and MJ. We're like family—sometimes we fight, but we always come back stronger. After *Shahs* ended, we kept talking about how our lives were evolving—new businesses, new relationships, new challenges. The San Fernando Valley became our backdrop, this vibrant place where we're balancing our Persian roots with the hustle of LA life. We knew getting another show off the ground would be a wild, tumultuous, and beautiful ride. This next chapter had already been years in the making. But we decided as a trio that we were up to the challenge and in fact excited to meet it head on.

Alex got it immediately: Our trio, plus a new generation of Persians, could bring something fresh yet nostalgic to Bravo. By November 2024, I was on Jeff Lewis's SiriusXM show spilling a little tea about a new project we were cooking up. GG, MJ, and I had been filming a pilot with a fresh crew of young, vibrant Persians, and we sent it off to Bravo with our fingers crossed.

By May 2025, Bravo gave us the green light, and *The Valley: Persian Style* (yeah, it's a working title) was born. It's not just a show—it's a celebration of who we are, where we come from, and where we're going. Most importantly, it's coming *from* us, not *to* us. We're diving into our culture, our friendships, and all the craziness of life in the Valley. I'm sure, looking ahead, that there will once again be moments where I'll have to remind myself and my friends and family that there are no fires burning. That no one is coming to get me or us. I imagine it's what someone feels like who is part of the mob but then finds a way to get out and goes into hiding. It's hard to get to a place where you can turn the key in the ignition, or press the button, and not flinch because you think the car might explode. But growing the courage to do it is the only way to get the car moving again and to get wherever it is you're meant to go.

Filming with GG and MJ again feels like coming home, but with a new energy. We're older, maybe a little wiser, but still serving the drama and laughs we know you'll love. This show is for us and for our fans who've been with us since *Shahs*, and for anyone ready to see Persian culture shine in a whole new way. Buckle up—you know with the three of us it's gonna be a hell of a ride.

ACKNOWLEDGMENTS

First and foremost, I want to thank my mother, who made me believe my dreams were within reach, and my father, who taught me how to lay the foundation for the life I'm living today.

This book wouldn't have been possible without the incredible talents and support of my team: my agents, Steve Troha and Katherine Odom-Tomchin at Folio; my editor, Kate Roddy at Sourcebooks; and Tony and Allie Baker for bringing my stories to life my way.

To my friends and chosen family—you are everything. My deepest gratitude to: Orly Marley, Arash Feyzjou, Atoosa Benji, Mercedeh Javid Feight, and Golnesa Gharachedaghi.

Last, but never least, thank you to my husband, Adam. Your support throughout this process, your encouragement to help me grow, and your constant reminder to be the "fun husband" means the world to me. I love you, Zetty.

And finally, to you—the readers and fans who have supported me, encouraged me, and given me the strength to navigate the emotions of this journey—thank you. This book is for you.

ABOUT THE AUTHOR

Reza Farahan is a charismatic TV personality, real estate mogul, and entrepreneur best known for his starring role on Bravo's hit reality series *Shahs of Sunset*. Born in Tehran, Iran, and raised in Beverly Hills, Reza has become an emblematic figure of resilience, humor, and unapologetic self-expression.

A proud Persian American and openly gay man, Reza has used his platform to challenge stereotypes, foster acceptance, and advocate for LGBTQ+ rights within the Middle Eastern community. With his quick wit and larger-than-life personality, he captivated audiences for nine seasons on *Shahs of Sunset*, chronicling his life, friendships, and the challenges of balancing cultural traditions with modern aspirations.